Engaging Children with Print

Engaging Children with Print

Building Early Literacy Skills through Quality Read-Alouds

Laura M. Justice

Amy E. Sofka

THE GUILFORD PRESS

New York   London

© 2010 The Guilford Press
A Division of Guilford Publications, Inc.
72 Spring Street, New York, NY 10012
www.guilford.com

Printed in the United States of America

This book is printed on acid-free paper.

Last digit is print number: 9   8   7   6   5   4   3   2   1

Library of Congress Cataloging-in-Publication Data

Justice, Laura M., 1968–
    Engaging children with print : building early literacy skills through quality
read-alouds / Laura M. Justice and Amy E. Sofka.
        p.   cm.
    Includes bibliographical references and index.
    ISBN 978-1-60623-535-5 (pbk. : alk. paper)
    ISBN 978-1-60623-536-2 (hardcover : alk. paper)
    1. Oral reading.   2. Reading (Early childhood)   3. Children—Books and reading.
  I. Sofka, Amy E.   II. Title.
    LB1573.5.J87 2010
    372.45′2—dc22
                                                                        2009049690

About the Authors

Laura M. Justice, PhD, is Professor in the School of Teaching and Learning, College of Education and Human Ecology, The Ohio State University. She has published nearly 100 articles, chapters, and reports on early education and language and literacy intervention, as well as 10 books. Dr. Justice is a recipient of the Editor's Award from the *American Journal of Speech–Language Pathology*; the Early Career Publication Award from the Council for Exceptional Children, Division for Research; and the Presidential Early Career Award in Science and Engineering from the United States government.

Amy E. Sofka, MEd, is presently serving as Project Director for two federally funded research studies: Preschool Experiences in Rural Classrooms (Project PERC) and Project Sit Together and Read (STAR), both conducted within the Center for the Advanced Study of Teaching and Learning at the University of Virginia. She has worked together with Dr. Justice on Project STAR since 2005. Ms. Sofka is the author of several articles and chapters describing approaches to supporting children's development within preschool settings, and has co-authored tools to assess teacher implementation of these approaches.

Preface

We have written this book to provide the public with materials generated through several federally funded research studies investigating ways to increase the emergent literacy skills of young children. For more than 10 years, members of our research team have examined ways to facilitate emergent literacy development in young children, using repeated readings of storybooks in ways that explicitly seek to foster children's engagement with print. In these various studies, we have generated and tested a lot of different materials; we envisioned this book as a means for disseminating the most user-friendly of those materials to the public.

We conceptualized this book largely as a means to bridge research-to-practice gaps that pose significant and real challenges to getting science into the hands of those who work daily with young children, including teachers, day care providers, speech–language pathologists, literacy coaches, social workers, and parents, among others. In so doing, this book is meant to be as accessible and usable as possible, including its summary of research support for the methods presented here; we refer those who desire greater detail to the research citations included throughout. We have included materials drawn from our research studies in the chapters and appendices, and we hope that these materials will be used effectively and liberally to foster young children's appreciation of, interest in, and engagement with print on a daily basis. By calling attention to print when reading with young children, adults can help children not only access but appreciate the world of print that surrounds them from infancy onward.

It is a popular wisdom among the American public that if every child were read to at least once every day, all children would enter school prepared for learning. We appreciate the sentiment, but more realistically believe that it is not simply reading a book to a child that matters most, but rather what that reading interaction looks like. As long as we are sitting to read with a child, let's ensure that we maximize the opportunities for learning that are taking place so that these interactions really can elevate children's long-term chances for academic success. This book is about how we can maximize these opportunities, and it helps one to do so by providing access to research-based findings regarding how, exactly, we can read to children in ways that will accelerate their emergent-literacy development over time.

ACKNOWLEDGMENTS

We are grateful for the involvement of many fine individuals in our research activities on reading books with children over the last 10 years. Those deserving very special mention (and in no particular order) include Helen Ezell, Joan Kaderavek, Aileen Hunt, Beth Cottone, Anita McGinty, Steve Petrill, Anita Bailie, Lori Skibbe, Ryan Bowles, Khara Pence, Xitao Fan, Rashaun Geter, Sonia Cabell, Tricia Zucker, Jill Pentimonti, Amelia Moody, Alice Wiggins, Marcia Invernizzi, Chris Lankford, Davida Parsons, Stephanie Curenton, Andrea Canning, Andrew Mashburn, Bridget Hamre, Robert Pianta, Allison Breit Smith, and Shayne Piasta. Many research assistants at the University of Virginia, The Ohio State University, and the University of Toledo have tirelessly helped to score and enter data, and their efforts deserve recognition. We also want to give a special "shout out" to Cathy Van Dyke, a research assistant at the University of Virginia who helped to assemble the book list in Appendix A. Adelaide Mykel, now age 7 years, also gets a hearty thanks for sharing with us the writing samples that appear in this book.

Over the last 10 years, financial support for our research has been provided by the American Speech–Language–Hearing Foundation, the U.S. Department of Education's Institute of Education Sciences, and the National Institutes of Health. We are grateful for this support.

We dedicate this book to the many school administrators, teachers, parents, and children who have participated in our research studies over the last 10 years. These individuals have given of their precious time for no reason other than to further our knowledge of what might help more children be successful in the pursuit of literacy. It is because of them—and we are deeply grateful—that we can be confident that the ideas and materials presented in this book have developmental benefits for young children.

Contents

Contents

CHAPTER 1

Entering a World of Print

Young Children's Development
of Print Knowledge

Children who are born into literate societies enter a world of print upon birth. Within hospital birthing centers, neonates are surrounded by doctors who write notes on clipboards; parents who read child-rearing manuals, parenting magazines, and survival guides; and grandparents who make entries in the blank pages of baby books. Furthermore, infants, toddlers, and preschoolers are raised in homes that are filled with books, magazines, shopping lists, coupons, and cookbooks, and they are cared for in day care centers and preschool programs that are filled with posters, signs, labels, calendars, schedules, and written rules. Although there are, of course, quantitative differences in the amount of print to which children in literate societies are exposed, as well as qualitative differences in the manner in which their interactions with print occur, few children today lead lives that are devoid of print. Indeed, children today live in a world of print and, even as very young children, the more they can engage with print as readers and writers, the more likely they are to experience academic and economic success. In fact, during the critical early years of development, from birth through kindergarten, the frequency and quality of children's early print experiences matter greatly in determining their future potential for becoming fluent readers and writers.

For many children, the development of print knowledge begins as early as birth, when they begin to take in the world around them by looking and listening during important early literacy activities. If children are read to as infants, their visual skills are developed enough for them to examine features of storybook illustrations, and their auditory skills are so refined that they can readily follow along with the voice of the caregiver as he or she reads a story. By 1 year, children may begin to recognize the difference between print and pictures as they look at the pages of storybooks on the laps of their parents, and perhaps even are producing proto-writing by scribbling with crayons on paper or even walls. By 2 and 3 years, children may recognize a few letters on billboards and signs in their environment, and likely are recognizing highly salient words that help them negotiate the world around them—such as their own names printed on their cubby at day care or the title of a favorite storybook. Even in these early years, children may begin to produce some writing of their own, often called *emergent writing*, providing explicit evidence that they are learning that print is a communication device. Figure 1.1 shows an emergent writing sample of 2.5-year-old Addie; this sample tells a story about Addie's cat and dog. Note the symbols and letters embedded in the picture, showing her awareness of printed units (in this case, the letters *d*, *b*, and *a* in particular) as having functional value.

In only a few short years, by 4 and 5 years of age, many children are reading some simple words in storybooks and on signs around them. They even may be producing words and stories in their own writing without the aid of an adult, with these emergent writings provided clear evidence of children's continually growing knowledge about both the forms and the functions of print. By age 5 and 6 years, in fact, children may be using print to serve many different functions or purposes; the examples of various functions served by print that children may learn about, as shown in Figures 1.2–1.9, were all produced spontaneously by Addie before or around her sixth birthday. Specific functions of print include:

FIGURE 1.1. Emergent writing produced by Addie at 2.5 years of age.

FIGURE 1.2. Addie's emergent writing (4 years): Letter address.

FIGURE 1.3. Addie's emergent writing (4.5 years): Postcard.

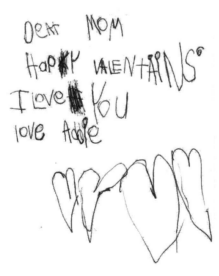

FIGURE 1.4. Addie's emergent writing (5 years): Holiday card.

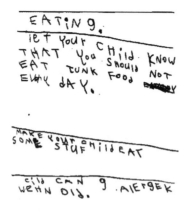

FIGURE 1.5. Addie's emergent writing (5 years): Research report.

FIGURE 1.6. Addie's emergent writing (5 years): List.

the girl

the mom

C'mon mom plese mom I'm beging you i want to!

FIGURE 1.7. Addie's emergent writing (5 years): Comic.

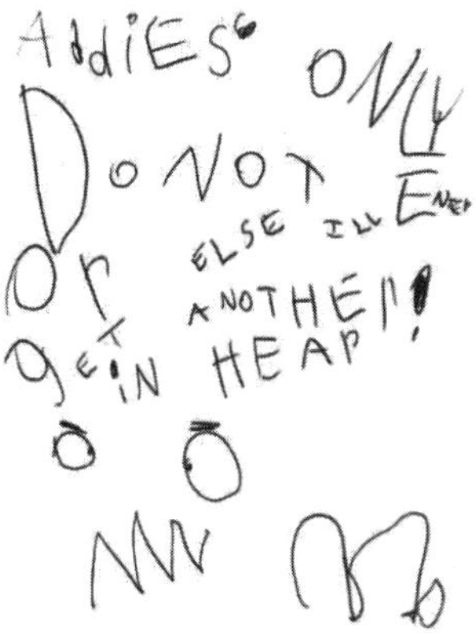

ADDIES ONLY DO NOT Or ELSE I'll ENd get ANOTHER IN HEAP!

FIGURE 1.8. Addie's emergent writing (5 years): Sign.

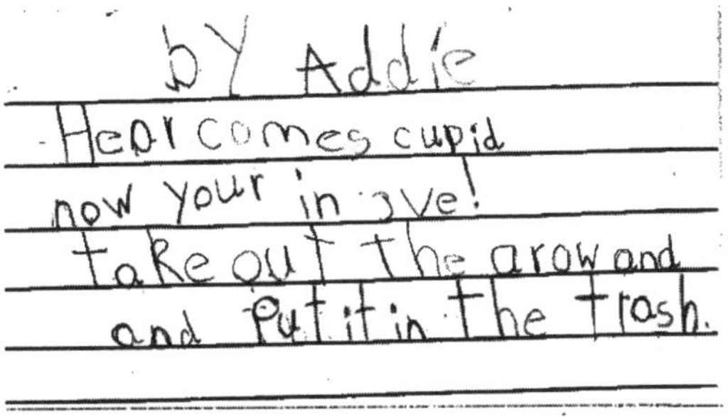

by Addie
Hear comes cupid
now your in 9ve!
take out the arow and
and put it in the trash.

FIGURE 1.9. Addie's emergent writing (6 years): Poem.

- Addressing a letter (Figure 1.2).

- Writing a postcard (Figure 1.3).

- Making a holiday card (Figure 1.4).

- Preparing a "research report" (Figure 1.5).

- Making a list (Figure 1.6).

- Creating a comic strip (Figure 1.7).

- Posting a sign (Figure 1.8).

- Writing a poem (Figure 1.9).

As these examples show, from birth through 6 years children are discovering the world of print that they have entered, and are rapidly accumulating knowledge of the functions and forms of print. They learn that their own productions of print can be used to inform, teach, warn, publicize, educate, greet, advocate, excite, and share with others. They learn that print produced by others serves all of these purposes as well, as they engage with print in storybooks, on signs, in magazines, and on posters. By *explicitly* and *intentionally* fostering young children's awareness of and interest in the print around them—in the home, in the classroom, and in the community—we can position children on an early and healthy trajectory of reading development and increase the likelihood that they will be active and lifelong consumers of the print around them.

In the remainder of this chapter, we provide an overview of children's earliest discoveries of and knowledge about print, drawing from empirical and theoretical research contributed by scholars in a range of disciplines. We then provide a brief overview of children's major achievements in print knowledge in the years of early childhood, describing specific achievements in four dimensions of print-knowledge development. Finally, we describe developmental and environmental factors that may place children at risk for inadequate development of print knowledge.

PRINT KNOWLEDGE: A WATERSHED EVENT IN READING DEVELOPMENT

Print knowledge is a *multidimensional* and *multidetermined* construct within the domain of early literacy development. The term *multidimensional* means that print knowledge captures not one but many different areas (or dimensions) of development, all of which concern children's developing knowledge about print. The term *multidetermined* means that print knowledge is influenced by both nature and nurture (biology and environment), or, put differently, by one's genes and environs.

This term *print knowledge* generally describes children's developing knowledge of two sets of characteristics regarding written language: its *forms* and its *functions* (Storch & Whitehurst, 2002; Whitehurst & Lonigan, 1998). The forms of written language include letters, words, and a range of different text structures (e.g., sentences, phrases, lists, stories, signs), as well as punctuation devices. Children's development of print knowledge includes learning not only these different forms, such as the analogous lower-case *a* and upper-case *A*, but also the rules that govern the use of case, such as the use of the need to capitalize the first letter at the start of a sentence. The rules that children must learn about print are similar, in many ways, to the rules young children must learn about oral language, such as how individual speech sounds are blended to create spoken syllables and words. Some examples of rules children will learn about print include these:

- Letters combine to form words.
- Letters come in analogous upper-case and lower-case formats.
- Words are the meaning-carrying units of written language.
- Letters and words are arranged left to right and top to bottom (in English).
- Spaces are used to differentiate words.
- Sentences begin with an upper-case letter and end with a punctuation unit.
- Proper names begin with upper-case letters.
- Reported speech is presented in quotation marks.

Some of these rules are learned incidentally during the years of early childhood as children experiment with writing and engage with storybooks and other texts under the guidance of others. For instance, a child may acquire knowledge of the rule that the personal pronoun *I*, when written, is always the upper-case letter *I* (and not the lower-case letter) as he helps to write a thank you note to his grandmother with close guidance from his mother. Within this incidental activity, the mother may even provide explicit guidance to her son about this rule:

MOTHER: I'll write this letter, but I need you to tell me what to say. Tell me what you want to say to Grandma.

ALEX: I love my bubble maker.

MOTHER: OK, so I'll write it like this. I am first going to make the word *I*. See, it's the letter *I*, write it just like this. Now *love*, that's *L-O-V-E*. Now *my*, *M*, and *Y*. And *bubble maker*. You do this part—draw a picture of the bubble maker here.

Children who do not have many incidental experiences with print, including those that are closely mediated by parents and other primary caregivers, may not learn many of the rules about print until they begin reading instruction in the primary grades. On the other hand, children who do have frequent opportunities to engage with print and to learn about its forms from more capable peers and parents often internalize this knowledge and have considerable familiarity with many of the rules that govern print well prior to beginning primary school.

In addition to learning rules about the forms of print, many children in the years of early childhood also develop sophisticated understandings about the functions of print. As with the rules about print forms, much of this knowledge is gained through relatively informal experiences with print under the guidance of others, including parents, siblings, friends, and early educators. The phrase *functions of print* refers to the many purposes that are served by print, which are identical to the functions served by spoken communication (i.e., speech). In a seminal work, Halliday (1975) differentiated the purposes of communication into seven different categories, or *communication functions*. These seven functions represent distinctive purposes for which humans communicate using spoken or written systems.

1. *Instrumental communication* is used to request something (e.g., "Can you buy milk?").

2. *Regulatory communication* is used to give directions and to direct others (e.g., "Go left onto Collins Drive.").

3. *Interactional communication* is used to converse and engage with others in a social way (e.g., "Who do you think will win the game?").

4. *Personal communication* is used to express a state of mind or feelings (e.g., "I am mad at you.").

5. *Heuristic communication* is used to request information and to inquire (e.g., "What time is it?").

6. *Imaginative communication* is used to tell stories and to roll play (e.g., "Once upon a time, there was a princess and a prince.").

7. *Informative communication* is used to provide an organized description of

an event or an object (e.g., "Right when the play started, the building began to shake because a train was going by ... ").

These seven basic functions of communication are necessary in developing and maintaining social relationships with other people, and for meeting our own basic needs and desires through speech or print. Even at very early ages, children use print to serve such basic functions. Which of the seven functions is represented in each of Addie's writing samples presented in Figures 1.2–1.9? Are any functions not represented?

In considering the young child's development of print knowledge—encompassing understandings about both the forms and functions of print—we can differentiate accomplishments into those representing skill development and those representing social practices or processes (Purcell-Gates, Jacobson, & Degener, 2004). *Skills*, as we use the term in this text, refer to the child's implicit and explicit knowledge of the written code, such as the names of individual letters and the combinatorial properties of letters into words, much of which is developed through implicit and explicit experiences both inside and outside of the classroom. Print knowledge, though, involves much more than a discreet set of skills. Print knowledge provides children with a set of tools that they will access throughout a lifetime as readers and writers to communicate with the world around them. Thus, print knowledge also involves the authentic social practices in which children engage as they experience and produce texts. Children's development of print knowledge involves a complex and synergistic interplay between skill development and social practice. As we emphasize throughout this book, teachers (as well as other adults who read often with children, such as parents) can use the social practice of storybook reading as a naturalistic and authentic interactive context in which to promote children's skill development in the area of print knowledge. Storybook reading is not the only social context in which children learn about print, however; therefore, many of the ideas presented in this book can be readily generalized to other literacy-learning contexts.

Print knowledge can be considered a *watershed event* in the child's development as a reader and writer. A watershed event is an important event upon which future developments depend. Children first must build a foundation of knowledge concerning how print works and what it does before they can achieve competence in unlocking the alphabetic principle and in comprehending the meaning of what they read, both of which are achievements typically accomplished in the primary grades. Without these basic understandings, children are likely to falter in the advent of formal reading instruction in the early primary grades. Indeed, we often describe the most pivotal watershed event in children's development as readers and writers as the development of *print interest*, wherein children become aware of and interested in the print within their environments (e.g., Justice & Ezell, 2004). With print interest, children begin to attend to and be interested in the print around them and to formulate and test hypotheses regarding the forms and functions of print. We can provide an authentic example by describing 24-month-old Griffin, the son of one of us (L. J.), who is read to nightly and is currently insisting that each session start with the storybook *Hug* by Jez Alborough. Griffin has just recently begun to demonstrate an explicit interest in print by pointing to and "reading" the title of the book (written in stark red writing in a speech bubble over a baby chimpanzee's head) in response to his mother's regular query ("Can you tell me the name of this book?"). Although for some time Griffin has been able to say the name of the book on demand, he has only now begun to associate the name of the book with the title printed on the cover page. L. J. is aware that his behavior is qualitatively different from that of only a few weeks prior, as he had never expressed any overt interest in or awareness of print in the book; now, with this emergent behavior, Griffin appears to be showing that he understands that print in the book carries a special function or purpose.

DIMENSIONS OF PRINT KNOWLEDGE

We noted earlier in this chapter that print knowledge is a multidimensional aspect of children's development. There are many skills, abilities, and behaviors that seem to reflect children's growing knowledge of print forms and functions. For instance, prior to entering the primary grades, a young child may do all of these things:

- Show an interest in the print that appears in the environment.
- Identify the title of favorite or familiar books.
- Follow along with one's finger when being read to.
- Recite the alphabet.
- Sing the alphabet song.
- Name some or all of the alphabet letters.
- Identify some letter–sound correspondences.
- Sign own name.
- Read some signs or logos in the environment.
- Read and write some common or familiar words.
- Prepare different written products (signs, letters, etc.).

- Identify the space between two written words.
- "Read" a book verbatim that is very familiar.

The above is only an abbreviated listing of the many skills, abilities, and behaviors that we may see as young children demonstrate their growing knowledge of print. Here we offer one way to organize and capture children's many developing skills, abilities, and behaviors in relation to print knowledge:

1. *Book and print organization*—knowledge of the ways in which print is organized in various texts.
2. *Print meaning*—knowledge of the functions of print as a communication device.
3. *Letters*—knowledge of the distinctive features and names of individual letters.
4. *Words*—knowledge of words as units of print that correspond to spoken language.

These four dimensions of knowledge collectively lay an important foundation for later achievements in both reading and spelling. Measurements collected of young children's knowledge across these different dimensions show that their cumulative knowledge about print is one of the more reliable and robust indicators of the ease with which they will progress as readers (Hammill, 2004; Morris, Bloodgood, Lomax, & Perney, 2003; Schatschneider, Fletcher, Francis, Carlson, & Foorman, 2004). We discuss these four dimensions in greater detail shortly.

Print knowledge is not only a multidimensional construct, as we have discussed, but it is also multi*determined*. This means that many different variables influence the development of print knowledge in young children, including both environment (nurture) and biology (nature). Recent studies of the print knowledge of monozygotic and dizygotic twins have helped to disentangle the relative impact of genetics and environmental factors on alphabet knowledge (Lemelin et al., 2007; Petrill, Deater-Deckard, Schatschneider, & Davis, 2005). Interestingly, these studies indicate that although genes are very important to reading development, the environments in which children are reared are also quite influential (Petrill et al., 2005). In fact, children's environment may have more influence on their development of print knowledge than other aspects of development, such as mathematical ability. What this means is that print knowledge is greatly influenced by the environments in which children are raised and, by extension, is an aspect of development that can be readily influenced by modifications to the environment.

Features of children's environments, including aspects of both home and school, directly influence their development of print knowledge. Within the home environment, these features include:

- Parental involvement in children's schoolwork and children's enjoyment of reading activities (Petrill et al., 2005).

- Parental beliefs concerning the importance and value of home literacy activities (Skibbe, Justice, McGinty, & Zucker, 2008).

- Frequency with which children are read books at home and in other caregiving environments (Sénéchal, LeFevre, Thomas, & Daley, 1998).

- Quality of book-sharing interactions between parents and children (McGinty & Justice, 2009).

Some aspects of children's schools that seem to affect their development of print knowledge include:

- Opportunity to participate in print-rich dramatic play experiences (Vukelich, 1994).

- Frequency with which children participate in shared writing activities (Aram & Biron, 2004).

- Frequency with which teachers talk about and point to print when they read books in the classroom (Justice, Kaderavek, Fan, Sofka, & Hunt, 2009).

Generally, research findings show that it is not simply the *frequency* or *quantity* with which children engage with print—during writing, reading, play, and other activities—that matters most to their development of print knowledge. Rather, it is the *quality* of these interactions, particularly the affective and interactive supports provided by caregivers as they scaffold children's learning about print that seem to be most influential to children's development (Roberts, Jurgens, & Burchinal, 2005).

PRINT-KNOWLEDGE ACHIEVEMENTS IN EARLY CHILDHOOD

Here we provide a general overview of children's major accomplishments in print knowledge that occur during the years of early childhood across the dimensions of *book and print organization, print meaning, letters,* and *words*. In discussing these achievements, we view children's development of print knowledge as following a *nonlinear trajectory* characterized by stops, starts, and slides. By way of illustration, let's consider two writing samples produced by Addie at 5 years of age. In Figure 1.8, note that Addie is producing a fairly complex writing in a sign prepared to post on her bedroom door. Her writing sample shows that she is mastering such written rules as left-to-right directionality, word spacing, and use of exclamation marks. Her spelling abilities are consistent with those of children in the early primary grades who are in a within-word-pattern stage of spelling development (see Bear, Invernizzi, Templeton, & Johnston, 2008, for description of primary-grade spelling patterns). In terms of social practice, Addie's intentions are clear in that she is producing writing that seeks to regulate the behaviors of others. Now, consider Addie's writing in Figure 1.10, collected at about the same time as the sample in Figure 1.8. What do you notice? The scribbling we see here, in which there are no recognizable letters and words and the function is decidedly unclear, seems like that of an emergent writer, perhaps one who is only 3 or 4 years of age. An informed observer who had no knowledge of Addie's writing abilities, as presented in Figure 1.8, might view her as immature in her writing ability, given her age. A more informed observer would consider the social circumstances in which Addie produced the sample in 1.10, in which she made it clear that she was going to practice her "cursive writing." As tempting as it is to use stage and phase models to illustrate children's developmental progression in early literacy development, as many experts do, we must recognize that children's growth may often resemble a more nonlinear pathway.

Moreover, we must also take care not to use age markers to dictate what children should be doing at a given point in time. Because much of children's print knowledge is experientially driven and reflective of experiences at home and in the community, we cannot attribute certain achievements to emergence

FIGURE 1.10. Addie's emergent writing (5 years): Practicing cursive writing.

at specific ages. It is tempting to attribute ages to specific achievements in early literacy development because of the close relationship between literacy and language development. In language development, many achievements—particular those within the domain of grammar—proceed along a fairly predictable timetable. For instance, most children say their first word at about 12 months of age and begin to produce two-word combinations (e.g., "Up, Mommy") at 18 months (Pence & Justice, 2007). Variability in language acquisition is more strongly mediated by genetics and heritability (i.e., nature) than occurs for literacy development, making achievements in print knowledge more variable because of the keen impact of environmental influences (Lemelin et al., 2007). Therefore, we simply cannot expect that most children will begin to write their name at 18 months of age in the same way that we can expect most children to begin to combine two spoken words into two-word utterances at this age.

Nonetheless, it can be valuable to understand the expectations that the sequence and timing of schooling within the United States place upon children in terms of arriving at school "ready to learn." As the terms *kindergarten readiness* and *school readiness* imply, there are parameters, influenced by cultural factors, that guide what educators and other professionals hope to see children doing and knowing at specific ages. Generally, these parameters place children along a continuum of *emergent* to *early* to *conventional literacy* that is based largely on when specific aspects of literacy are taught and learned, as shown in Figure 1.11. What is important to recognize is that timing matters greatly, in that the instructional focus in the early primary grades is based upon the presumption that children arrive with some understanding of print and sound. Children who arrive with these understandings in place will be able to respond to the targets and techniques of more formal reading instruction, whereas those children who do not have these understandings in place may fail to keep up. We discuss here some of the specific accomplishments we often see among young children in the four dimensions of print knowledge mentioned previously.

Book and Print Organization

Book and print organization is the dimension of print knowledge that concerns children's understanding of how books and other types of texts are organized. The knowledge children acquire about book and print organization during the years of early childhood typically includes learning about (1) the title of book, (2) the author of book, (3) page order, (4) page organization, and (5) print direction, as presented below. Note that the descriptions below are specific to languages such as English and Spanish, in which words and sentences are printed from left to right, and may not be applicable to other languages that do not use this pattern.

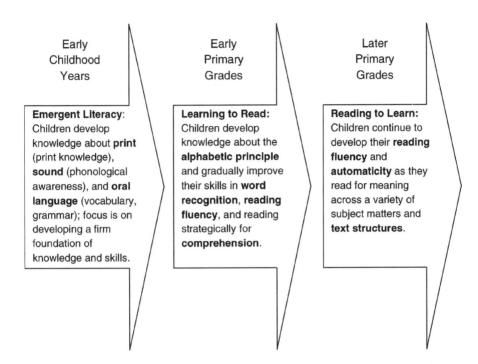

FIGURE 1.11. Literacy learning and teaching continuum.

1. *Title of book*. Knowledge of where the title is located in a book (on the cover and the title page, typically) and what the function of the title is.

2. *Author of book*. Knowledge of what an author is and where the name of the author is located in a book (on the cover and the title page, typically); this category also includes children's knowledge of the role of the illustrator.

3. *Page order*. Knowledge of how books are read from front to back and that pages are read from left to right in a two-page spread.

4. *Page organization* (top and bottom). Knowledge of how a page with multiple lines of text is read from top to bottom.

5. *Print direction*. Knowledge of how print moves from left to right.

Print Meaning

Print meaning is the dimension of print knowledge that concerns children's understanding of the functions or roles of print. The knowledge children acquire about print meaning during the years of early childhood typically includes learning about (1) the function of print, (2) environmental print, and (3) the concept of reading, as presented below.

1. *Function of print.* Knowledge that the purpose of print generally is to convey meaning.

2. *Environmental print.* Knowledge about the specific and varying purposes served by print within the environment (on signs, logos, posters, etc.).

3. *Concept of reading.* Knowledge that reading is an act in which persons engage for various purposes.

Letters

Letters comprise the dimension of print knowledge that concerns children's understanding of the functions and forms of the letters of the alphabet. The knowledge children acquire about letters during the years of early childhood typically includes (1) upper- and lower-case formats, (2) letter names, and (3) metalinguistic concepts of letter, as presented below.

1. *Upper- and lower-case forms.* Knowledge that letters come in two analogous forms and that there are rules governing when the forms are used.

2. *Letter names.* Knowledge of the names and corresponding written symbols for the 26 individual letters.

3. *Concept of letter.* Knowledge of the functions of letters: that these are units of print that correspond to sounds and are organized to build words.

Words

Words comprise the dimension of print knowledge that concerns children's understanding of the functions and forms of written words. The knowledge children acquire about words during the years of early childhood typically includes (1) concept of word in print, (2) short words versus long words, (3) letters versus words, and (4) word identification, as presented below.

1. *Concept of words in print.* Knowledge that written words, as a distinct unit of print, correspond to spoken words.

2. *Short words and long words.* Knowledge that written words are a distinct unit of print that are composed of varying numbers letters (some with many letters and others with few letters).

3. *Letters and words.* Knowledge that written words are distinct from the other salient form of print (letters) and that words have meaning.

4. *Word identification.* Knowledge of some words in print, including one's own name and other high-frequency or high-function words.

In the remainder of this book we describe to educators how they can intentionally build children's knowledge across these multiple dimensions, summarized in Table 1.1, by calling attention to print during storybook reading interactions. In fact, we provide very specific guidance on how to create a storybook reading program that systematically builds children's knowledge and skills across these four dimensions of knowledge. In the next chapter we discuss the research behind the approach we describe.

FOSTERING YOUNG CHILDREN'S ACHIEVEMENTS
IN PRINT KNOWLEDGE: WHY AND HOW?

In this book we emphasize specific ways in which teachers and others, including parents, can use storybook-reading interactions as a means to strategically and systematically support young children's development of print knowledge. This is not to say that storybook-reading interactions do not and cannot be used to foster many other critical domains of development; on the contrary! Research findings make it quite clear that children's growth across multiple developmental domains can be fostered through their frequent engagement in high-quality storybook readings with adults, particularly domains of language development. For instance, by participating often in high-quality read-aloud experiences, children show increases in their grammatical comprehension and their vocabulary knowledge (e.g., Lonigan, Anthony, Bloomfield, Dyer, & Samwell, 1999; Whitehurst et al., 1988). In this text, however, our interest is specifically focused on how storybooks can be used to build children's knowledge of print—an important goal for many young children today.

Promoting young children's achievements in print knowledge throughout the emergent literacy years is important for several fundamental reasons. First, print knowledge is an important precursor to and foundation for later achievements in beginning reading (as children learn to read) and advanced reading (as children read to learn) (see Figure 1.11). Children who do not have this foundation in place may struggle in beginning reading instruction, which, in turn, can compromise their success in more advanced reading activities. In contrast, children who bring to beginning instruction a solid knowledge of the forms and functions of print will find it relatively easy to learn to read (Storch & Whitehurst, 2002).

Second, the development of print knowledge can be greatly compromised by the presence of a developmental disability. For instance, children who in the preschool years exhibit a language disorder typically have much less knowledge about print compared to children who do not have a language disorder (Justice,

TABLE 1.1. Early Childhood Achievements in Four Dimensions of Print Knowledge

Book and print organization

Title of book	Knowledge of where the title is located in a book (on the cover and the title page, typically) and what the function of the title is
Author of book	Knowledge of what an author is and where the name of the author is located in a book (on the cover and the title page, typically); this category also includes children's knowledge of the role of the illustrator
Page order	Knowledge of how books are read from front to back and that pages are read from left to right in a two-page spread
Page organization	Knowledge of how a page with multiple lines of text is read from top to bottom
Print direction	Knowledge of how print moves from left to right

Print meaning

Function of print	Knowledge that the function of print generally is to convey meaning
Environmental print	Knowledge about the specific and varying functions served by print within the environment (on signs, logos, posters, etc.)
Concept of reading	Knowledge that reading is an act in which persons engage for various purposes

Letters

Upper- and lower-case forms	Knowledge that letters come in two analogous forms and that there are rules governing when the two forms are used
Letter names	Knowledge of the names and corresponding written symbols for the 26 individual letters
Concept of letter	Knowledge about the functions of letters: that these are units of print that correspond to sounds and are organized to build words

Words

Concept of words in print	Knowledge that written words, as a distinct unit of print, correspond to spoken words
Short words and long words	Knowledge that written words are a distinct unit of print that are composed of varying numbers of letters (some with many letters and others with few letters)
Letters and words	Knowledge that written words are distinct from the other salient form of print (letters) and that words have meaning
Word identification	Knowledge of some words in print, including one's own name and other high-frequency or high-function words

Bowles, & Skibbe, 2006), and as many as one-half of preschoolers with language disorders will later exhibit a reading disability (Catts, Fey, Tomblin, & Zhang, 2002). It is unclear as to why children experiencing language disabilities have less knowledge about print compared to others; some researchers theorize that it occurs due to a combination of factors that include both experiential issues (e.g., less frequent participation in book-reading interactions) coupled with developmental difficulties that make learning about written language particularly challenging (e.g., challenges processing linguistic stimuli) (McGinty & Justice, 2009). Nonetheless, it seems likely that limited print knowledge at the start of beginning reading instruction is at least partly to blame for these adverse outcomes for children with language disorder, because it is very difficult to catch up in reading development following a slow start (Skibbe et al., 2008).

The presence of a disability is not the only circumstance that can compromise development of print knowledge, however. Children who are reared in poverty also tend to exhibit much less knowledge about print compared to children reared in more advantageous circumstances (Justice et al., 2006). This might occur because of limited resources within the home environment (e.g., storybooks) or perhaps because parents' emotional resources are directed toward addressing basic family needs (e.g., securing food, maintaining shelter). Among children reared in poverty the risks for becoming a poor reader are very well documented and constitute a significant policy issue in the educational arena (Snow, Burns, & Griffin, 1998). Efforts to accelerate the earliest literacy achievements of children reared in poverty are currently viewed as one of the more effective mechanisms for preventing reading difficulties among at-risk children (Snow et al., 1998). Experts believe that by giving young children a healthy early advantage in literacy development, as occurs by systematically building their understandings about and interest in print during the preschool years, the incidence of reading difficulty among children at risk due to poverty will be greatly reduced.

In this book we present a scientifically based approach for building children's early knowledge about print; this approach draws upon one of the most comfortable, familiar, and common routines of early childhood: namely, the adult–child book-reading interaction. Although many teachers and other professionals (e.g., speech–language pathologists) may use storybook-reading interactions within the classroom as a venue for supporting children's language achievements, they may not be aware of how storybooks can be used intentionally and systematically to build children's knowledge about print. In the remainder of this text we describe in detail how teachers and others can harness the power of the book-reading routine to systematically and explicitly promote children's knowledge about print across the four key dimensions: book and print organization, print meaning, letters, and words. Teachers can do this by the simple strategy of *calling attention to print* as they read. This strategy involves pointing to and talking about print on the pages of the book as we read with children—it's as simple as that! In Chapter 2 we provide specific details of research findings showing that adult–child reading interactions that feature an explicit focus on print, which occurs when adults call attention to print, substantially accelerates the development of print knowledge of children, including those who are at risk for future reading difficulties due to disability and/or poverty.

Fostering Children's Engagement with Print

Chapter 1 provided the foundation for understanding the importance of print knowledge as a critical component of children's emergent literacy development. We discussed four dimensions of print-knowledge development: book and print organization, print meaning, words, and letters. Children increase their understandings across these four dimensions of print knowledge through a variety of early childhood literacy activities *that feature the guidance of more knowledgeable partners*, including parents and teachers. The importance of the guidance that parents, teachers, and other adults provide to children as they participate in various childhood literacy activities cannot be underestimated; indeed, it is not the literacy activity that matters most in the effect to develop children's knowledge about print, but the mediation that adults provide to foster this knowledge. Figure 2.1 depicts the role of adults as mediators of children's understandings, and emphasizes a key research finding in the last decade showing that a critical determinant of children's print knowledge is the frequency with which other people explicitly mediate their interactions with print. By *explicitly mediate,* we refer to instances in which children are engaging with print and an adult (or even sibling or friend) helps them to internalize and understand specific features and functions of that print. Let's look at an example of explicit mediation:

MOTHER: This book is called *Spot Bakes a Cake*. We haven't read this one before.

SANDI (3 years): But we read a different one about Spot's school.

MOTHER: That's right. We have read the book about Spot going to school. This one's called *Spot Bakes a Cake*. That's the title right there. Do you know this word (*pointing to the word* Spot)?

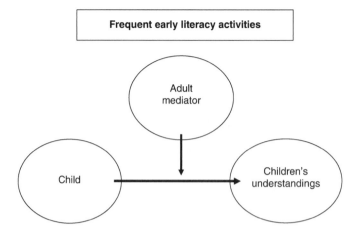

FIGURE 2.1. Adults as mediators of children's understandings in early literacy activities.

SANDI: Yep, that says Spot (*pointing to the word* Spot).

MOTHER: Wow, you're right. I guess you've seen that word. Let's try to do all the words. Read them with me, OK?

SANDI AND MOTHER: (*in unison as the mother points to each word in the title*) *Spot ... bakes ... a ... cake.*

The above scenario provides a clear demonstration of explicit mediation in its depiction of the mother's intentional guidance as she helps her child not only focus on and be aware of words on the cover of this storybook, but also to view them as an object of her attention. The mother mediates the child's interactions with the print and, in doing so, helps to focus the child's attention on the print within the book. In the simplest terms, the mother has helped the child to have *contact with print* in this reading exchange. We know that the child has had contact with print because she is most certainly looking at the print and she is talking about the print. Let's contrast Sandi's experience in this interaction with another one, in which she is being read the same storybook at day care:

Teacher: This book is *Spot Bakes a Cake.* Sandi brought this to school today and said we could read it. This looks very good! It looks like Spot is going to make a cake in this one. Let's see what happens. (*Opens book to the first page and reads text on the first page.*) I was right. They are going to make a cake for Dad's birthday. What kind of cake do you think they'll make?

CHILDREN: (*Call out various options.*)

TEACHER: I think it will be chocolate. We'll have to find out. (*Turns the page and reads text on the next page.*)

Like Sandi's mother, the teacher here has the important role of mediating children's experiences with the text; however, what is important to notice is that the teacher does not use any specific behaviors or techniques that serve to focus children's attention on the print within the book. The teacher does not explicitly mediate the children's interactions with print in this exchange. In fact, the behaviors of this teacher, if we view adults as mediators of what children experience during book-reading and other activities, have actually resulted in the children having *no contact with print* in this reading exchange. Whereas Sandi, when reading the same storybook with her mother, appeared to have a great deal of contact with print in the book, when the children are read this book by their teacher, they seem to have no or very little contact with the print. As we discuss later in this chapter, such differences can have very large impacts on children's development of print knowledge. Children who are read storybooks in ways that do not support their contact with print will show little growth in development of print knowledge even if they are read to repeatedly; on the contrary, children who are read storybooks in ways that explicitly support their contact with print will show tremendous growth in print knowledge over time.

In this chapter we discuss how adults can read storybooks with children in ways that increase their contact with the written language within storybooks. We discuss, in particular, how adults can use a technique we describe as *calling attention to print,* to not only increase children's interaction with print but, in turn, improve their knowledge about print. It is important to recognize that when the adult calls children's attention to print contained within storybooks, he or she is, in fact, directing their attention toward the *written language*—or the written representation of spoken language. Because of this intersection between spoken and written language, directing children's attention toward print should not detract from the positive oral language experiences that are typically attributed to the shared storybook reading context (e.g., Whitehurst et al., 1988). Rather, by explicitly directing children's attention toward written language in the book, the adult is seeking to create synergies among children's development of both oral and written language: By learning more about written language, children's general language abilities are enhanced rather than reduced.

This chapter introduces this technique and, as importantly, describes the scientific evidence that supports teachers' and others' use of this technique.

Today, educators are pressed to use instructional techniques that are empirically validated and evidence-based (Stanovich & Stanovich, 2003); for this reason, it is important to share details on research findings that support educators' use of calling attention to print.

CALLING ATTENTION TO PRINT

As we look at the differences in the amount of explicit mediation Sandi's mother and teacher provide that may influence Sandi's contact with print, what we notice is that Sandi's mother is overtly *calling attention to print*, whereas Sandi's teacher is not. We use the phrase *calling attention to print* to capture the many different behaviors adults who read with young children can use to increase children's focus on print. Generally, calling attention to print involves adult use of both *verbal references to print* and *nonverbal references to print* (Justice & Ezell, 2000, 2004):

- *Verbal references to print* are adult verbal behaviors, such as questions and comments about print, that increase children's contact with print during book-reading and other literacy activities. Some types of verbal references are *evocative*, in that they explicitly seek to engage children in conversations or question–answer exchanges about print. Other verbal references are *nonevocative*, in that they seek to provide children with information about print. Questions about print are generally evocative, whereas comments about print are generally nonevocative.

- *Nonverbal references to print* are adult nonverbal behaviors, such as tracking the print when reading (running one's finger under the words simultaneous to reading them) and pointing to print, that increase children's contact with print during book-reading and other literacy activities.

Table 2.1 provides a description of these two techniques used to call attention to print, as well as some examples. Later in this book, we describe how these techniques can be combined with the domains of print knowledge discussed in Chapter 1 (book and print organization, print meaning, letters, and words) to create a systematic approach to promoting print knowledge within the early education classroom.

Now we focus on the evidence showing the great benefits children experience when they read books with adults who call attention to print. Perhaps the

TABLE 2.1. References to Print

General techniques	Specific types	Examples
Verbal references	Questions about print	"What do you think this says here?" "Do you know this letter?"
	Comments about print	"This says 'Danger!'" "This letter is an *S*, like your name."
	Requests about print	"Show me where I should read." "Point to the words as I read."
Nonverbal references	Points to print	*Adult points to specific letters, words, or other features of print in the book.*
	Tracks the print	*Adult tracks the narrative text with finger while reading.*

Note. Adapted from Justice and Ezell (2004). Copyright 2004 by the American–Speech–Language–Hearing Association. Adapted by permission.

most straightforward benefit is that children come to notice print, which is a very important and necessary accomplishment on the pathway to becoming a reader. In fact, without first noticing print, children cannot begin to learn more about it. Consider the findings from research showing that adult use of verbal and nonverbal references to print substantially increases young children's contact with print when they are read storybooks (Evans, Williamson, & Pursoo, 2008; Justice, Pullen, & Pence, 2008). For instance, when adults use nonverbal references to print—tracking the print and pointing to print in illustrations—4-year-old children look at the print in storybooks almost twice as much as they do when adults do not use any nonverbal references to print (Justice et al., 2008). Figure 2.2 shows differences in the number of times children look at print when they are read to in three different ways: with no references to print, with verbal references to print (questions and comments about print), and with nonverbal references to print (tracking and pointing to print).

As the data in Figure 2.2 show, when adults read storybooks to preschoolers and simply read the text and talk about the illustrations, children fixate on print about 11 times during the entire reading event; however, when adults read the same storybooks and include nonverbal references to print, children fixate on print about 21 times during the event. These differences can add up dramatically over time. If we extrapolate these findings to typical preschool children who are read to for 10 minutes per day for an entire year, children who are read to by adults who nonverbally reference print by tracking the print and pointing to print will fixate on print about 40,000 times during these reading experiences compared to about 20,000 fixations on print for children who are read to by

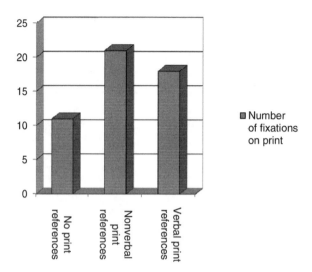

FIGURE 2.2. Number of fixations on print by 4-year-old children when read to three different ways. Adapted from Justice, Pullen, and Pence (2008). Copyright 2008 by the American Psychological Association. Adapted by permission.

adults who seldom or never nonverbally reference print (Justice et al., 2008). Not surprisingly, children who look more often at print during storybook-reading experiences have more knowledge about print compared to children who seldom look at print (Evans et al., 2008).

Figure 2.3 provides a general schema for understanding the role that adults can play in explicitly mediating children's contact with print within the book-reading context. Although seemingly a simple model, the propositions contained within it have far-reaching implications. That is, we and others have found, in more than a decade of research, that adults—parents, early childhood educators, and other professionals who work with young children—have a very important role to play in determining how much direct contact with print children experience within the shared book-reading context. And, as importantly, when adults increase children's contact with print within the shared book-reading context, children will experience significant gains in their print knowledge. Related to this point, and to fully understand the proposition we are making, there are three major findings in the scientific literature that warrant discussion:

1. Children have little contact with print during prototypical shared book-reading experiences.

2. Adults can readily increase children's contact with print by calling atten-

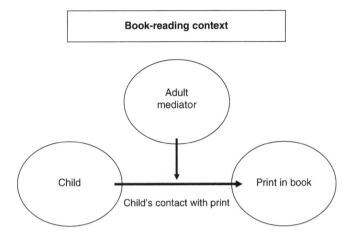

FIGURE 2.3. Adult as mediator of child's contact with print.

tion to print during shared book-reading experiences, using verbal and nonverbal references.

3. Children who have increased contact with print during shared book-reading experiences because adults call attention to print experience an acceleration in their development of print knowledge.

Figure 2.4 provides an illustration of the second and third of these findings, namely how differences in adults' attention to print can influence children's contact with print within the book-reading experience, which, in turn, can influence children's learning about print within this context. In Scenario 1, adults' use of calling attention to print—that is, talking about print and pointing to it (e.g., as Sandi's mother did early in this chapter)—can give a child a great deal of contact with print in the reading context and thus many opportunities to develop knowledge about forms and functions of print. On the other hand, in Scenario 2, adults' limited use of calling attention to print can result in a child having no or very little contact with print in the reading context and, as a result, no opportunity to develop knowledge about the forms and functions of print.

In the remainder of this chapter, we provide additional details on the evidence available to support the three scientific findings listed above, namely, that (1) children have little contact with print during prototypical shared book-reading experiences; (2) adults can readily increase children's contact with print by calling attention to it during shared book-reading experiences by using verbal and nonverbal print references to it; and (3) children who have increased contact

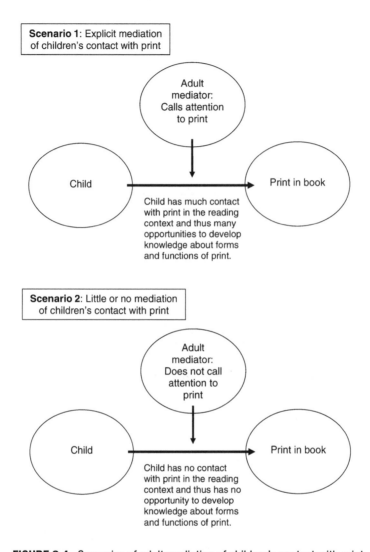

FIGURE 2.4. Scenarios of adult mediation of children's contact with print.

with print during shared book-reading experiences because adults call attention to print experience an acceleration in their development of print knowledge.

FINDING 1: CHILDREN HAVE LITTLE CONTACT WITH PRINT DURING PROTOTYPICAL SHARED BOOK-READING EXPERIENCES

Researchers and educators have long viewed storybook-reading experiences as one of the more fertile contexts of early childhood in which children develop key understandings about print forms and functions (e.g., Snow, 1983). A number of more recent scientific papers have raised questions, however, about how much children actually learn about print when they are read books (Justice, Skibbe, Canning, & Langford, 2005; Yaden, Smolkin, & Conlon, 1989). These researchers have focused specifically on children who are in the emergent literacy period of development, particularly the later preschool years (when children are 3–5 years of age), and have sought to determine the extent to which children extract knowledge about print from reading experiences. A particularly perplexing finding in this body of work involved evidence of very low correlations (correlations signify the strength of a relationship between two variables) between the *frequency* of book-reading experiences in children's home and children's *knowledge about print* (e.g., Sénéchal et al., 1998). In light of prevalent theories that children develop knowledge about print forms and functions within the book-reading context, findings showing there to be a low or no relationship between the frequency of book-reading experiences and children's print knowledge are quite confounding. That is, if we assume that children learn a lot about print when they are read books, we would assume there to be at least a modest correlation between measures of frequency of book-reading experiences in children's homes and children's print knowledge. Instead, research has shown the relationship to be surprisingly low.

Such perplexing findings have led researchers to look much more closely at the nature of children's book-reading experiences in the home and elsewhere, including the preschool classroom. What, in fact, is the prototypical book-reading experience, and can we find any evidence to show that children are, in fact, learning about print when they are read storybooks? An interesting body of evidence has emerged in the last decade to show, fairly consistently, that when young children are read storybooks, they have *very little contact with print*. Rather, it seems that when children are read to in the years of early childhood, they have contact, nearly exclusively, with pictures in the book. Consider, for instance, that researchers have shown that children rarely talk about print or look at print when they are read to (Evans et al., 2008; Ezell & Justice, 2000; Justice et al., 2008). Similarly, researchers have also shown that adults reading with children (parents, teachers, and other key caregivers) rarely talk about print, nor do they make print an overt object of attention by using nonverbal references to print, such as tracking the print when reading (Ezell & Justice, 2000; Hammett, van Kleeck, & Huberty, 2003; Phillips & McNaughton, 1990). Such findings help us to understand why there appears to be no substantial relationship between the frequency with which children are read to and their knowledge about print (since, for many children, shared book-reading experiences do not seem to help them learn about print).

Let's look at a few of these findings in greater detail to illustrate these points. First, let's consider a research study conducted by Hammett and colleagues (2003) that involved examining the verbal reading behaviors of 96 parents (65% mothers, 35% fathers) as they read storybooks with their 3- and 4-year-old children. As part of their study, the researchers transcribed every utterance produced by parents during the reading interactions and then coded them based on content. One specific code was used to denote print/book conventions, that is, parent utterances that referenced print in some manner. Overall, parent references to print represented about 12% of their utterances, which suggests that parents provided their children reasonable opportunities to learn about and attend to features of print during the reading exchanges. However, if we look a bit more closely at the data, we find that only a small minority of mothers and fathers (9 of the 96) is producing nearly all of these verbal references to print; in fact, these parents produce an average of 11 verbal references to print per book reading session. References to print occur at much lower rates for the other parents. In fact, the majority of parents (two-thirds of the sample) reference print only a few times when they read books with their children. Hammett and her colleagues' research shows us that, yes, a small minority of parents do explicitly foster their children's verbal interactions with print during reading interactions, but the majority of parents do not.

Second, let's consider a research study conducted by Ezell and Justice (2000), which produced findings similar to those of Hammett and colleagues. We wanted to determine how often adults reading to young children referenced print verbally *and* nonverbally; moreover, we also wanted to determine how often children talked about print when reading storybooks with adults that contain very interesting print features. This study involved videotaping and then coding the reading interactions of 24 female speech–language pathology graduate students, all of whom were quite experienced in working with children, as they read storybooks to 4-year-olds. The book they read was *Spot Bakes a Cake* (Hill, 1994), which was selected because it contains numerous interesting print features, such as speech bubbles attached to characters on nearly every page, as well as print embedded within the pictures (e.g., on one page, Spot's mother is holding a shopping list with legible words printed on it). The reading behaviors of the speech–language pathology students were coded to indicate the occurrence of five specific types of print references:

1. *Questions about print.* Adult production of questions that reference print in the storybook (e.g., "Do you know this letter?").
2. *Requests about print.* Adult production of directives or imperatives that reference print in the storybook (e.g., "Look at the words on that sign.").

3. *Comments about print.* Adult production of comments that reference print in the storybook (e.g., "This sign says *Danger.*").

4. *Tracking the print.* Adult runs finger along the narrative text while reading.

5. *Pointing to print.* Adult points to letters or words in narrative text or in illustrations.

The occurrence for each of these types of print references was carefully coded by the research team for each adult reader; then, the frequency of occurrence for each was divided by the length of reading sessions to determine the rate with which the adult readers used each of the five types of print references. These rates are presented graphically in Figure 2.5. As you can see from these data, each of these types of print references, with the possible exception of tracking the print, occurred at very low rates. For instance, the adults produced, on average, 0.15 questions about print and 0.71 comments about print per minute of reading. If adult verbal references to print serve to mediate children's contact with print, one can presume that the children reading storybooks with these adults had relatively little contact with print. Analysis of the amount of

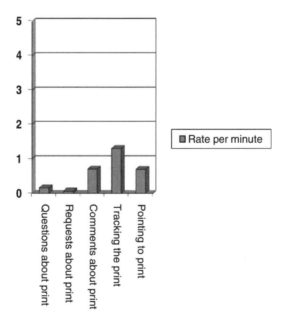

FIGURE 2.5. Rate (per minute of reading) with which adults use verbal and nonverbal print references. Adapted from Ezell and Justice (2000). Copyright 2000 by the American Speech–Language–Hearing Association. Adapted by permission.

comments and questions about print the children themselves produced support this point. When children's utterances were coded as to whether they referenced print or some other feature of the storybooks, such as illustrations, less than 4% of children's utterances referred to print. These findings paint a similar illustration of the prototypical storybook-reading interaction that preschool-age children experience as that suggested by Hammett and colleagues' findings: that children have little contact with print when they are read books by adults.

Third, as one final piece of evidence to round out this point, let's consider recent findings from research studies that have actually documented what children are looking at when they read books with adults. Evans and Saint-Aubin (2005) involved 10 four-year-old children in a study that sought to identify how much time children actually look at print when they are read storybooks. The children were developing typically in all regards, even with respect to literacy; for instance, they knew an average of 8 of the 26 alphabet letters. What the children looked at when they were read storybooks was determined using an eye-gaze camera, a tool that can document exactly how much time a child visually fixates on different regions of the pages in a book (e.g., fixations on pictures vs. print in this study). On average, children were found to spend about 4% of the time looking at the storybook fixating on print compared to 96% of time fixating on pictures. The researchers concluded from their findings that "it is difficult to see how shared reading, without additional explicit references to the print within the books, can be a major vehicle for developing children's … print-specific skills" (Evans & Saint-Aubin, 2005, p. 918).

There are, of course, some parents and teachers who do foster children's contact with print within book-reading experiences by making additional explicit references to the print, and the evidence suggests that this has positive benefits for children. This is an important finding because it provides early educators with an opportunity to modify their typical reading behaviors in ways that can improve children's developing understandings about print. We turn to these findings now.

FINDING 2: ADULTS CAN INCREASE CHILDREN'S CONTACT WITH PRINT BY CALLING ATTENTION TO IT

In the previous section we noted that many children have generally little contact with print when they are read storybooks. In the prototypical reading experience, children rarely look at print or talk about print, and the adults with whom they read rarely point to print, comment about it, or ask a question about it. Nonetheless, it is quite simple for adults to increase their efforts to draw children's attention to print through nonverbal behaviors, such as pointing to print, and verbal behaviors, such as commenting on and asking questions about print. And, when they do so, children's contact with print increases. Let's consider some of the scientific evidence showing this to be the case. We'll look at two studies, the first investigating children's talk about print as an index of their contact with it, and the second considering children's visual attention to print as an index of their contact with it.

We previously discussed a study by Ezell and Justice (2000) that sought to determine how often adults reading to young children referenced print verbally and nonverbally. Recall that this study involved coding the reading interactions of speech–language pathology graduate students as they read the storybook *Spot Bakes a Cake* (Hill, 1994) to 4-year-old children. Although this book contains numerous interesting print features, such as speech bubbles, the researchers found that the speech–language pathology students rarely made any verbal or nonverbal references to print (see Figure 2.5). The specific types of print references coded included (1) questions about print, (2) requests about print, (3) comments about print, (4) tracking the print, and (5) pointing to print. Perhaps because the adults in this study rarely referenced print, the children who were being read to made very few utterances (only 4%) about the print in the storybook either.

In this same study we also sought to determine what would happen if the adults increased their efforts to draw children's attention to print—that is, would it increase children's talk about print? Of the 24 graduate students involved in this study, 12 were randomly assigned to watch a videotape that modeled for them how to incorporate verbal and nonverbal print references into their reading interactions with young children. This 7-minute video featured vignettes of a mother reading to her preschool-age son, and, as she read, she incorporated both verbal (commenting and questioning) and nonverbal (pointing, tracking) references to print into the reading interaction. After the graduate students watched the video, they were asked to read the storybook *Spot Bakes a Cake* to the same children they had read to previously. Interestingly, in this second reading, they greatly increased their verbal and nonverbal references to print, as shown in Figure 2.6. As importantly, the children with whom they read the storybook also showed a significant increase in their comments about print, as depicted in Figure 2.7. Specifically, when the children were read storybooks by adults who made verbal and nonverbal references to print, about one in four (25%) of children's utterances related to the print within the storybook. This is a substantial increase over the 4% of child utterances concerning print that was seen when children were read storybooks by the same adults when making very few verbal and nonverbal references to print. This finding reveals that *children follow the adult's lead in terms of what aspects of the book are worthy of discussion*—in short,

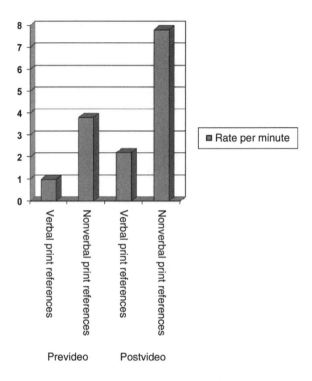

FIGURE 2.6. Rate (per minute of reading) with which adults use verbal and nonverbal print references before (pre) and after (post) viewing a video of parent use of print references. Adapted from Ezell and Justice (2000). Copyright 2000 by the American Speech–Language–Hearing Association. Adapted by permission.

If adults do not reference print, neither do children. However, if adults make print an object of attention by referencing it through verbal and nonverbal means, children too will make print an object of their attention.

A more recent study addressed the same issue; namely, to determine whether children's attention to print would increase as a function of adults' use of verbal and nonverbal references to print (Justice et al., 2008). This study differed from the study discussed in the prior paragraph, however, in that it focused on what children *look at* when they are read storybooks and whether their visual attention to print would increase in response to adult references to print. Researchers determined the percentage of fixations focused on print versus pictures when 4-year-old children were read storybooks in four different styles:

- *Verbatim reading.* The adult reads the storybook straight through and does not use any verbal or nonverbal references to draw attention to print, pictures, or the story line.
- *Picture-focused reading.* The adult reads the storybook and asks questions

and makes comments about the illustrations (e.g., "Oh, look, Spot is wearing a costume.").

- *Print-focused reading: nonverbal print references.* The adult reads the storybook and nonverbally references print by tracking the narrative text while reading and pointing to print embedded within illustrations (e.g., speech bubbles of characters).

- *Print-focused reading: verbal print references.* The adult reads the storybook and verbally references print by asking questions and making comments and requests about print forms and functions (e.g., "Oh, look, this letter, *S*, is in your name!").

Figure 2.8 notes the percentage of children's fixations on print (vs. other material on the page, primarily pictures) within the storybooks for these four types of reading styles. This figure shows that children looked at print almost twice as often when adults used a reading style that involved pointing to and tracking the print (print-focused reading style: nonverbal print references) or asking questions and making comments and requests about print forms and functions (print-focused reading style: verbal print references). The authors of this study point out that these differences can add up over time. For instance, if a child is read to for just 10 minutes a day for 1 year using a picture-focused reading style, he or she will look at print an estimated 20,000 times; however,

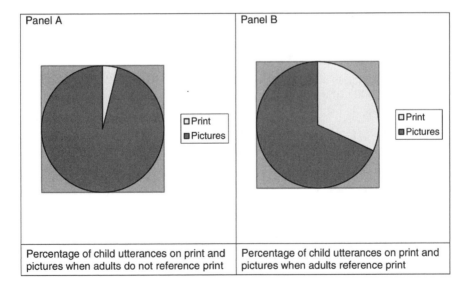

FIGURE 2.7. Amount of child talk about print when adults reading to them do not reference print (Panel A) and do reference print (Panel B). Adapted from Ezell and Justice (2000). Copyright 2000 by the American Speech–Language–Hearing Association. Adapted by permission.

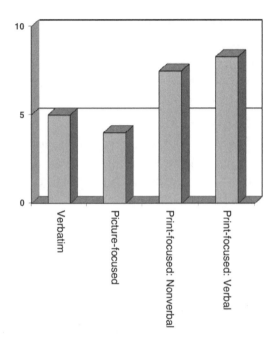

FIGURE 2.8. Percentage of fixations on print (out of total fixations) by 4-year-old children when being read storybooks in four different styles. Adapted from Justice, Pullen, and Pence (2008). Copyright 2008 by the American Psychological Association. Adapted by permission.

if that same child is read to for 10 minutes a day for one year using a print-focused reading style, he or she will look at print nearly 40,000 times. Consider also that the differences become even more dramatic if children are read to for 30 minutes a day, with children read to using a print-focused style looking at print nearly 60,000 times more than children read to using a picture-focused reading style. Because the number of times children look at print within story-books is associated with how much they know about print (Evans et al., 2008), these differences may have important implications for understanding why some preschool-age children have little knowledge about print whereas others have quite sophisticated knowledge.

FINDING 3: WHEN ADULTS CALL ATTENTION TO PRINT, CHILDREN'S DEVELOPMENT OF PRINT KNOWLEDGE ACCELERATES

Thus far in this chapter we have presented scientific findings showing that young children generally have little contact with print when they are read storybooks

(Finding 1), but that adults can increase children's contact with print by using nonverbal and verbal references to print, which, in turn, increase children's talk about print and visual attention to print during reading interactions (Finding 2). A reasonable question to ask, however, is whether increases in children's talk about print and visual attention to print actually leads to increases in children's *print knowledge*. In Chapter 1 we discussed how *print knowledge* is an important area of emergent literacy development that refers to children's developing knowledge about the forms and functions of print. Specific accomplishments in print knowledge typically observed among children in the emergent literacy period of development include:

1. *Book and print organization*—knowledge of the ways in which print is organized in various texts.

2. *Print meaning*—knowledge of the functions of print as a communication device.

3. *Letters*—knowledge of the distinctive features and names of individual letters.

4. *Words*—knowledge of words as units of print that correspond to spoken language.

We also discussed in Chapter 1 how some children, including children with disabilities and those reared in poverty, can experience a slow start in their development of knowledge about print. In turn, this slow start can compromise their likelihood of success as they learn to read and read to learn. Because this may serve an important mechanism for preventing later reading difficulties, researchers have increasingly become invested in determining effective ways by which to accelerate young children's learning about print. One particularly effective approach, which is described in greater detail later in this book, involves adult use of verbal and nonverbal references to print when reading books with young children, what we refer to as *calling attention to print*. Research findings have consistently shown that *when adults call attention to print, children's development of print knowledge accelerates*.

Table 2.2 provides an overview of six studies which have found positive benefits of adult use of print referencing when reading books with young children, and we provide details concerning several of these research studies here. Specifically, in this section we provide details of findings from three studies showing the benefits of calling attention to print (verbal and nonverbal print referencing) as used by parents (Study 1), speech–language pathologists (Study 2), and teachers (Study 3). Collectively, these studies show that children's development

TABLE 2.2. Studies Examining the Effects of Calling Attention to Print/Print Referencing

Study	Adult readers	Child participants	Length	Context
Ezell, Justice, & Parsons (2000)	Parents	4 children with communication disorders	5 weeks (four readings per week)	1:1 reading at home
Justice & Ezell (2000)	Parents	28 typically developing children	4 weeks (four readings per week)	1:1 reading at home
Justice & Ezell (2002)	Speech–language pathologists	30 children from economically stressed homes	8 weeks (three readings per week)	Small groups at preschool
Justice, Kaderavek, Fan, Sofka, & Hunt (2009)	Teachers	106 children from economically stressed homes	30 weeks (four readings per week)	Large groups at preschool
Justice, Skibbe, McGinty, Piasta, & Petrill (2008)	Parents	29 children with language disorders	12 weeks (four readings per week)	1:1 reading at home
Lovelace & Stewart (2007)	Speech–language pathologists	5 children with language disorders	13 weeks (two readings per week)	1:1 reading at preschool

of print knowledge is accelerated when adults who read books with them make print an object of focus within the reading interactions.

Parents as Readers

When parents incorporate verbal and nonverbal references to print into their shared reading interactions with their preschool-age children, the children's knowledge of print increases dramatically. Justice and Ezell (2000) demonstrated this in a study of 28 parents (largely middle class) who read a set of eight storybooks to their 3- to 5-year-old children over a 4-week period; in total, parents read to their children 16 times in one-on-one reading sessions. Each parent was given the same set of eight storybooks to use in the home reading sessions, and all storybooks had interesting print features embedded within the illustrations (e.g., speech bubbles, font changes, labeled illustrations).

Half of the parents were asked to incorporate verbal and nonverbal references to print into their reading sessions, whereas the other half were told to read as they normally read to their children. Researchers tested the children prior to and following the 4-week reading period on four measures of print knowledge. Compared to children who were read to by parents using their normal reading style, those who were read to by parents in a print-referencing style experienced dramatic gains on two measures (the dimensions of print and book organization and words), modest gains on one measure (the dimension of print meaning), and no gains on one measure (the dimension of letters). A comparison of print-knowledge gains across the two groups of children is presented in Figure 2.9. An important finding from this work is that relatively modest changes in parents' reading style could result in fairly dramatic improvements in some aspects of children's print knowledge. Indeed, the acceleration of children's print knowledge presented in Figure 2.9 occurred after only 4 weeks of home reading.

Speech–Language Pathologists as Readers

Children who have disabilities, by many accounts, experience a slow start in the development of print knowledge. This is particularly true for children who have a language-learning impairment, given the close relationship between language and literacy development (Justice et al., 2006). Children with language disorders often experience a slow start in development of print knowledge which, in turn, can negatively impact the likelihood that they will achieve success in the future years of reading development. Consequently, it is important to consider ways to accelerate emergent literacy learning among children with disabilities who experience early delays in literacy development. On the basis of the prom-

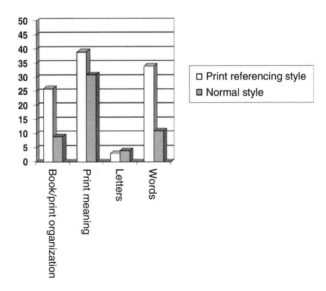

FIGURE 2.9. Gains on four measures of print knowledge for children whose parents used a print referencing style versus a normal style. Adapted from Justice and Ezell (2000). Copyright 2000 by the American Speech–Language–Hearing Association. Adapted by permission.

ising findings with regard to parent use of print referencing in the home environment, researchers have considered whether use of this technique as applied within preschool settings can have benefits for children with disabilities.

In one such study, researchers Lovelace and Stewart (2007) incorporated a storybook reading that featured print referencing into the one-on-one speech–language therapy sessions provided to five children with language disorders. The intervention sessions were conducted for children over 13 weeks (two sessions per week) in children's preschool classrooms. Each child received a one-on-one therapy session that lasted about 30 minutes twice per week; in the last 10 minutes of the session, the therapist would read a storybook with the child and would comment about print, point to print, and track the print while reading. A total of 20 specific print concepts were highlighted using these types of print references (e.g., location of the title of the book, left-to-right directionality of print). A close examination of performance patterns across the five children showed that all exhibited increases in their knowledge of the targeted print concepts over the 13-week therapy program. The authors found that children learned some print concepts more easily than others; for instance, all children learned how a page was organized (e.g., the difference between the top and bottom of a page) and the role of the illustrator of a book, but none learned what a letter is. An interesting finding in this study was that speech–language pathologists can incorporate print referencing into their therapy sessions with children with disabilities, and that this inclusion can result in accelerated emergent literacy growth for children facing risks in the area of reading.

Teachers as Readers

Reading books with children is a ubiquitous aspect of the daily routine in the preschool classroom. In many classrooms, children have the opportunity to participate in reading interactions with adults multiple times across the day. It is perhaps a surprise that studies of how teachers read books to preschool children indicate that relatively little attention is focused on print (e.g., Zucker, Justice, & Piasta, 2009). Nonetheless, it is also true that if teachers make print an interesting and relevant part of the storybook reading routine by explicitly calling attention to it through verbal and nonverbal references, children show substantial benefits.

Consider the findings from a recent study of 23 teachers who worked in preschool programs serving children from economically stressed homes (Justice et al., 2009). In this study, teachers received a new book each week for 30 weeks to read to their children four times in a large-group setting. In total, children participated in 120 reading sessions over the course of an academic year. Nine of the teachers in this study were told to read the storybooks each week using their normal style of reading. By contrast, the other 14 teachers received training at the start of the year on how to call attention to print when reading the target storybooks, and each book they read was linked to specific print-related topics to talk about. For instance, when reading the first book of the year—*My First Day of School* (Hallinan, 1987)—teachers were asked to talk about *environmental print* and *concept of reading*; these topics were presented previously in Table 1-1 as achievements in the print-knowledge dimensions of print meaning. To help the teachers incorporate these topics into their reading sessions, a card accompanied each book that described the topics and gave guidance on how to make these topics an object of conversation when reading particular books. The card teachers received that accompanied *My First Day of School* is presented in Figure 2.10; note that it is two-sided, with one topic per side.

There are a few interesting findings from this study to report. The first concerns teachers' reading behaviors, particularly the extent to which teachers verbally referenced print when reading to children. Figure 2.11 provides a comparison of the number of times teachers in the two groups (those who were trained to read with a print referencing style vs. those who read with their normal reading style) verbally referenced print across the four dimensions: print and book organization, print meaning, letters, and words. Generally, teachers who read with their normal reading style referenced print at only very low rates; instead, teachers largely referenced features of illustrations. By contrast, teachers who were trained to read with a print referencing style addressed three of the four dimensions of print at much higher rates. This finding is interesting because it shows that preschool teachers who read with their normal reading style seldom reference print, but that teachers can readily incorporate attention to print if trained to do so.

The second interesting finding concerns what happens to children's print knowledge when their teachers read with a print referencing style, especially as compared to children whose teachers read with their normal reading style. Approximately six children in each of the 23 classrooms were individually assessed in the fall and the spring of the academic year—before and after the 30-week reading program was implemented by teachers in their classrooms. Two measures used to assess children's knowledge of print included (1) *alphabet knowledge* (the number of letters children can correctly identify) and (2) *print concepts* (the number of print concepts children can correctly identify). Figure 2.12 provides a comparison of children's gains on these two measures between the fall and spring of the year; as the data in this figure show, children whose teachers read to them with a print referencing style showed a substantial acceleration of print knowledge related to children whose teachers read with their normal

My First Day of School

TARGET: Environmental Print

★ **High-Support Examples**

1) TECHNIQUE: MODELING THE ANSWER

Teacher: We see words and letters at the bottom of this page. Who can show me where we see words and letters somewhere else?

Child: Here? (*Points to tray of food.*)

Teacher: Almost. Here, here are some letters and words on the cereal box. (*Reads Snappy Snax, then moves to calendar and bread bag.*)

2) TECHNIQUE: ELICITING THE ANSWER

Teacher: This sign says "Safety First!" Can anyone tell me what this sign says?

Child: Safety First!

Teacher: That is exactly right! The sign says "Safety First."

★ **Low-Support Examples**

1) TECHNIQUE: ENCOURAGEMENT

Teacher: Who can find the *W* on this page? William, I think you can find it since you know how to spell your name.

William: Up here?

Teacher: You got it! That is the letter *W*, just like in *William* and *Wanda*.

2) TECHNIQUE: EXPLANATION

Teacher: Can anyone read what this sign says?

Child: *Stop!*

Teacher: You knew that! Yes, this sign says *Stop*. You see this sign on the road when you are riding in the car.

STAR: **Sit Together and Read**

(side 1)

My First Day of School

TARGET: Concept of Reading

★ **High-Support Examples**

1) TECHNIQUE: MODELING THE ANSWER

Teacher: This book is called *My First Day of School*. I can't wait to read this book. I think we are going to learn about being at school on the first day, and maybe about meeting new friends, too. What else are we going to learn?

Child: Look at the pictures of the boy!

Teacher: We will look at pictures of the boy, and we're going to *read* it, and learn all kinds of things about school and being there on the first day. You guys know all about this, but now we'll read about it, too.

2) TECHNIQUE: ELICITING THE ANSWER

Teacher: This book is titled *My First Day of School*. This book is about things that happen on the first day of school. What do you think this story is about?

Child: Riding a bus!

Teacher: I think you're right. Riding a bus is something many of you do on the first day of school. I think we'll learn other things about the first day, too.

★ **Low-Support Examples**

1) TECHNIQUE: PREDICTION

Teacher: Today we're going to read this book. Look at the cover. What do you think we'll learn from reading this book?

Child: About school?

Teacher: Yes, I think so too. We'll learn about things that happen at school.

2) TECHNIQUE: RELATING TO THE CHILD'S EXPERIENCE

Teacher: Let's look at this picture. I think these must look familiar to you. Can anyone tell us what this page teaches us?

Child: It looks like the place where I put my stuff.

Teacher: Exactly. I think this page will remind us to keep things neat and clean in our room.

STAR: **Sit Together and Read**

(side 2)

FIGURE 2.10. Print target card (two-sided) for storybook *My First Day of School* (Hallinan, 1987).

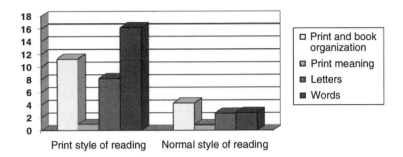

FIGURE 2.11. Two groups of preschool teachers' verbal references to print (across four dimensions) at winter observation. Adapted from Zucker, Justice, and Piasta (2009). Copyright by the American Speech–Language–Hearing Association. Adapted by permission.

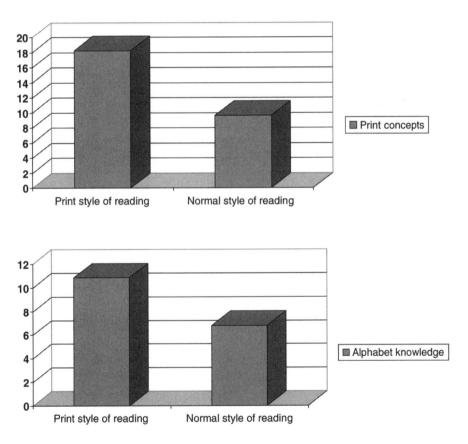

FIGURE 2.12. Children's gains on measures of print concepts and alphabet knowledge when read to with print referencing versus normal style of reading. Adapted from Justice, Kaderavek, Fan, Sofka, and Hunt (2009). Copyright 2009 by the American Speech–Language–Hearing Association. Adapted by permission.

reading style. The results of this study provide convincing evidence that *when adults call attention to print, children's development of print knowledge accelerates.*

In the remainder of this book, we provide guidance on how to systematically and explicitly enhance children's knowledge about print by calling attention to it within the context of adult–child storybook reading interactions. As the research findings reviewed in this chapter make clear, anyone can use the approach we describe—not only teachers, but also parents, speech–language pathologists, and others. Because one of the most essential ingredients of this approach is the interaction that takes place between adult and child when sharing a book, we now turn to describing the book-reading context in general terms, with a focus on creating high-quality interactions in which children are invested in learning.

CHAPTER 3

Calling Attention to Print
The Nuts and Bolts

Now that we have provided a basic overview of young children's development of print knowledge (Chapter 1) and scientific evidence concerning what happens when adults increase children's contact with print during storybook-reading interactions (Chapter 2), we turn our attention to the nuts and bolts of the technique we refer to as *calling attention to print*. In Chapter 2 we noted that this term captures the many different behaviors that adults can use to increase children's contact with and awareness of print and its meanings. Generally, adults call attention to print through a combination of verbal (e.g., questioning about print) and nonverbal (e.g., tracking the print) references. Children's increased engagement with, and attention to, print leads to substantially improved knowledge about the forms and features of print; these foundational emergent literacy skills (i.e., print knowledge) are strong predictors of later success in reading (National Early Literacy Panel, 2008). Therefore, by calling attention to print *now* when you read with young children, you are supporting their future outcomes as readers.

As discussed in Chapter 2, a number of studies on calling attention to print has been conducted over the last decade. From this body of work, we have learned a great deal regarding how best to use the technique of calling attention to print to foster children's print-knowledge development; these are the nuts and bolts of the approach, and they concern such issues as how best to sequence instruction over time (sequence of instruction) and how often to use this technique (intensity of instruction). In this chapter we discuss the following specific nuts and bolts:

1. Context of instruction
2. Scope of instruction

3. Sequence of instruction

4. Intensity of instruction

One important issue—a "bolt" so critical it holds the whole reading session together—concerns the choice of books used when calling attention to print. This is such an important topic that it receives its own chapter (Chapter 4), in which we specifically discuss not only how to select books but also how to link these selections with specific print targets. Additionally, how to scaffold children's participation in reading sessions that feature a print focus is also a highly important topic which we address in considerable depth in Chapter 5.

CONTEXT OF INSTRUCTION

Context refers to the environment in which something takes place, and with respect to calling attention to print, it refers to the shared book-reading context. The shared book-reading context is a rapidly changing, or *dynamic*, environment in which adults and children interact with one another to derive meaning from the text being shared. The adult reader, in particular, must maintain a highly active role to assure that throughout the entire length of the reading session, all children are fully engaged, enjoying, and learning from the activity; in this regard, the adult's role is particularly crucial and can be highly challenging. We use the term *intentional* to describe the adult who plays a highly active role for the purposes of facilitating children's engagement, enjoyment, and learning from the shared reading activity: The intentional reader uses a variety of techniques simultaneously to achieve these ends.

Understanding the various techniques with which adult readers create highly productive and successful reading sessions with children is necessary if we are to then integrate attention to print within the reading context. That is, if calling attention to print is to be an effective technique for increasing children's knowledge about print, then it must be situated in an enticing and engaging context in which the adult reader intentionally ensures that children are actively engaged as participants. The way in which the adult reader—for instance, the preschool teacher—organizes and facilitates the shared reading session is particularly crucial for ensuring that the context in which calling attention to print takes place maximizes children's engagement, because children who are highly engaged benefit more strongly from participating in shared reading sessions than children who are disengaged (Justice, Chow, Capellini, Flanigan, & Colton, 2003). Figure 3.1 provides an overview of seven unique aspects of the book-reading context to which adult readers must carefully attend in order to

Reader: _____ Text: _____

Observer: _____ Date: _____

1 = Item not present, inconsistently executed, or poorly executed   3 = Item present and strongly, skillfully executed

2 = Item present and adequately executed

Scale	Description	1 (Low)	2 (Mid)	3 (High)	Comments
Orientation	Introduces the book through display of the book cover, reading of title, author, and illustrator. Encourages discussion of one or more of these features. Links the book, author, or subject with children's prior knowledge.				
Physical Delivery	Posture, facial expressions, pausing, and voice changes (frequency, intensity) are used to capture and maintain children's attention.				
Word Learning	Discusses interesting words before, during, and/or after the reading of the book aloud. Uses pictures, where possible, to support the discussion.				
Language Elicitation	Asks open-ended questions (e.g., "what if," "where have you seen," "how would") to prompt discussion of book, details of plot and/or characters, or topic. Regularly pauses and encourages the children to fill in the predictable phrases. Extends and recasts children's contributions with follow-up comments and questions that maintain children's topic (topic continuations). Elicits participation of reticent children.				
Responsiveness	Is responsive to the individual needs of children and tries to involve all children equally. Is responsive to the experiences and knowledge of individual children that may contribute to the reading experience. Allows children to share their feelings and experiences and listens attentively and respectfully.				
Behavior Management	Proactively manages behavior (e.g., selects appropriate group size, sets appropriate pace, situates children in appropriate places), and little time is focused on managing behavior. Establishes "ground rules" for how children are to participate early in the session and is consistent throughout in enforcing these rules.				
Extension	Prompts children to relate what was read to events outside the book, linking the book's text and the children's experiences. Involves children in activities that extend the book (e.g., story map, retelling, role playing).				

FIGURE 3.1. Reading Quality Scale.

purposefully create high-quality reading contexts. Note that the Reading Quality Scale presented in Figure 3.1 does not explicitly address attention to print; we first want to describe broader features of a quality reading session, in which attention to print is then systematically and explicitly embedded.

Orientation

Orientation refers to techniques the adult reader uses to set the stage and prime children's engagement before any reading takes place. These include showing children the book and identifying its general topic (e.g., the first day of school), as well as key features of the cover (author, illustrator, title, cover art). Beyond this, the orientation provides an ideal context to engage in focused discussions about (1) background knowledge, (2) prior experiences with the book, (3) book predictions, and (4) story grammar. The orientation provides an ideal opportunity for elevating children's background knowledge (also called prior knowledge) about the topic, particularly if it is novel to them. For instance, if a book describes a family who harvests a field, orientation might include a discussion of the meaning of the word *harvest* and, ideally, reference to experiences children have had relevant to this concept (e.g., a prior visit to an apple farm).

If children are being read a book with which they are familiar, discussing prior experiences with and perceptions about the book is also an important aspect of the orientation. The reader might allow children to discuss what they remember about the book (e.g., something interesting about the character) or identify something specific that they particularly enjoyed about it. A survey is helpful in this regard: A highly successful orientation activity might ask children to sign their names under one of three columns, each of which identifies something specific about the book content, to signify which aspect of the content they most enjoyed.

A common routine with respect to orientation is asking children to predict what might happen in the book. Predictions can be made for both familiar and unfamiliar books. Prediction is an important orientation activity because it fosters children's inferential thinking skills, which are very important later in school when children need to read for meaning and call upon inferencing abilities to do so successfully. Adult readers can structure prediction activities used to orient children to a book by allowing each child to make a prediction and write it down on a white board or large sheet of paper; this structure is useful because it provides a written account of children's predictions to which the adult can refer during the reading of the book (with periodic checks for accuracy of children's predictions) or after the reading, when each child's prediction can be checked in succession.

Some adults may use orientation as a time to prime children's awareness of features of story grammar. Traditional elements of story grammar include the setting, characters, plot, and conclusion. The adult reader can use an activity to orient children toward one or more of these features of a book's story grammar prior to reading the book. For instance, the adult might explain to children that the story is set in a highly peculiar place and they are to pay special attention as he or she reads because they will be talking about the setting of the story after the reading is completed.

Physical Delivery

The physical delivery of a book concerns how the adult uses paralinguistic communication devices to excite and engage children as the book is read. Paralinguistic communication devices are aspects of communication that accompany and surround the actual words we use, such as posture, facial expressions, pauses, and voice changes that include modifications in pitch (frequency) and loudness (intensity). Some books seem particularly amenable to pitch and loudness modifications, such as books that feature different characters that likely vary in their voices. Adults should use these book elements as an opportunity to explore physical delivery variations. It is surprising how powerful such techniques can be when used well by readers as a means for drawing children into a reading experience and maintaining their attention throughout.

Word Learning

Reading books with children offers a significant means to foster their vocabulary growth. *Vocabulary* refers to the volume of words that children understand (receptive vocabulary) and express (expressive vocabulary), and by many accounts, early childhood is a particularly robust period in life for vocabulary acquisition. Books provide an important source of new words to which to expose young children, particularly words that are relatively low in frequency but high in utility. A lower-frequency word is one that occurs relatively rarely in spoken language (e.g., *toddler, knob, holler*), whereas a high-frequency word occurs relatively often (e.g., *boy, button, call*). High-utility words are words that are *useful* to mature language users—words that we must use and understand to read for meaning and engage in conversations with others and that are used in many different contexts (e.g., *fragile, whisper, reside*) (Beck, McKeown, & Kucan, 2002).

When reading books with young children, it is useful to take opportunities to explicitly explore and discuss interesting lower-frequency words that occur in books. Examples of such interesting lower-frequency words appearing in Anne

Hunter's (1998) *Possum and the Peeper* include *inconsiderate, demand, clamor, din, snarl, grumble, glorious,* and *warm.* Any one of these words is ripe for conversation, yet often adults reading books with children will simply read them and move on, providing children with no opportunity to derive the meaning of these words. Because these are words that occur relatively less often than others, it may be some time before the words are heard again, thus limiting children's opportunity to acquire their meaning and make them part of their emerging vocabularies.

When these words occur in books, adults should take a moment to pause and explore the meaning of these words with children, using a technique described as an "elaborated exposure"; that is, explicitly pointing out an interesting vocabulary word to children and discussing its meaning in child-friendly language (Beck et al., 2002; Justice, Meier, & Walpole, 2005). For instance, a teacher might elaborate on the word *inconsiderate* in this way:

> *"Inconsiderate* is an interesting word. It means that someone is rude or not very thoughtful. Someone in this book is making really loud sounds, and the animals think that is rude, or inconsiderate. Let's say the word *inconsiderate* together: *inconsiderate."*

Because this word refers to a relatively abstract concept, it may take several exposures to its definition before children are able to describe it in their own words. The next time the teacher reads the book and pauses to discuss this word, he or she might ask children to define it in their own words.

Some adult readers may choose not to interrupt their reading of books with children to elaborate interesting words within the context of the story. This is certainly understandable. However, in such cases, opportunities to discuss interesting words should not be abandoned altogether; rather, they can occur before or after the book reading as an orientation or extension activity.

Language Elicitation

A high-quality reading session involves opportunities for children to actively participate in the dialogue that occurs. Particularly useful strategies for eliciting children's participation in dialogues include asking open-ended questions (questions that elicit multiword responses, such as, "Why are the animals angry about all the noise?"), pausing and waiting, providing opportunities for children to fill in predictable words, and extending children's contributions with comments or questions that maintain the children's topic of interest (topic continuations). Equally important is ensuring the verbal participation of children who are reticent, perhaps because of their temperament (i.e., shyness), cultural background, or language abilities. As with pointing out interesting words, some adult readers may feel uncomfortable dialoguing with children during the actual reading of the text; instead, they prefer to hold conversations before or after reading so as not to interrupt the flow of the story. Such a preference is certainly acceptable, as long as the adult ensures that children do not miss the opportunity to discuss the story in extended dialogues.

Responsiveness

A significant characteristic of high-quality reading sessions is that of adult responsiveness: The adult uses specific behaviors to show that he or she is linguistically and emotionally attuned to the individual interests and needs of the children. Adults are linguistically responsive when they repeat and extend children's communicative contributions, as in:

> CHILD: That monkey in the jungle ...
>
> ADULT READER: Yes, the monkey is hiding in the jungle.

The adult response is appropriately characterized as linguistically responsive because he or she (1) *recasts* the child's utterance (i.e., repeating a child utterance and embellishing it with additional grammatical detail) *and* (2) *maintains* the child's topic. Linguistic responsiveness is an important means for facilitating children's language growth and encouraging their conversational participation (e.g., Landry, Miller-Loncar, Smith, & Swank, 1997); the previous item on the Reading Quality Scale (Language Elicitation) captures adult readers' use of recasts and topic-maintaining utterances.

In addition to linguistic responsiveness, an important element of quality book-reading sessions is emotional attunement to individual children—attunement to their interests, their approaches to learning, and their ability to stay engaged, for instance. This characteristic is sometimes referred to as sensitivity. The adult reader who is sensitive (or emotionally responsive) recognizes when children need help or special attention and expresses interest when children share their ideas and interests (Pianta, La Paro, & Hamre, 2004).

Behavior Management

A well-managed book-reading session is a productive one, with as little time as possible focused on managing children's behaviors, particularly those that disrupt the reading experience. Ideally, any behavior management that needs to take place can be proactive in manner through such actions as (1) selecting the appropriate group size, (2) setting the appropriate pace, and (3) situating children in appropriate places. For instance, a child who is extremely fidgety and has a tendency to poke nearby children may need to sit right in front of an adult reader. An important characteristic of a well-managed book-reading session also involves preset expectations; that is, the adult reader establishes his or her expectations for child behavior before the reading session and then maintains these expectations throughout. As an example, a preschool teacher may want to explain to children that because the group of children listening to a book is so large, they will need to raise their hand (rather than call out) in order to answer questions. It is important that this rule be enforced equally for all children and that the teacher use some sort of gesture (e.g., holding up a hand or a picture of the desired behavior) to let children know when they haven't followed the rule rather than stopping the session repeatedly to reprimand children.

Extensions

Extensions are follow-up activities that lengthen the book-reading experience for children by building on specific themes or concepts. Extensions can immediately follow a book-reading experience (e.g., digging a garden after reading a book about a garden), but they do not need to. For instance, a teacher might be on a field trip to a play with preschoolers and remind the children that they once read the book on which the play is based; perhaps prior to the start of the play, the teacher could help children remember the major story grammar elements of the book they shared previously. Extensions can be a particularly important way for children to repeatedly experience new vocabulary words they learned within the context of a book. For instance, an extension activity might involve children producing kid-friendly definitions for 10 interesting words heard within a storybook (Biemiller & Boote, 2006).

SCOPE OF INSTRUCTION

Calling attention to print involves using books as a means to foster not only children's interest in print as an object in the world around them, but also to systematically teach children about print. In the preceding sections we discussed key features of high-quality shared reading sessions, such as language elicitation and adult responsiveness, that must be in place for children to appreciate and learn from reading experiences. Once these are in place, adults can then draw upon the enticing and engaging experience of repeatedly reading books with children to systematically develop their knowledge about print.

In Chapter 1 we described four dimensions of print knowledge that capture children's achievements over the course of early childhood:

1. Book and print organization.
2. Print meaning.
3. Letters.
4. Words.

These dimensions can be used to represent a fourfold scope of print-knowledge instruction that, in turn, can be systematically addressed by calling attention to print during shared reading interactions. Here, we provide a brief review of the definitions of these four dimensions of print knowledge and the major accomplishments within each, which in turn can serve as specific *targets* or *objectives* to be addressed by calling attention to print.

Book and Print Organization

The five objectives for print instruction include:

1. *Title of book.* Knowledge of where the title is located in a book and what the function of the title is.
2. *Author of book.* Knowledge of what an author is and where the name of the author is located in a book.
3. *Page order.* Knowledge of how books are read from front to back and that pages are read from left to right.
4. *Page organization.* Knowledge of how a page with multiple lines of text is read from top to bottom.
5. *Print direction.* Knowledge of how print in English moves from left to right.

Print Meaning

The three objectives representative of this dimension of print knowledge include:

1. *Function of print.* Knowledge that the function of print generally is to convey meaning.
2. *Environmental print.* Knowledge about the specific and varying functions served by print within the environment.

3. *Concept of reading.* Knowledge that reading is an act in which persons engage and that reading serves various purposes (e.g., learning new things, enjoyment).

Letters

Three objectives represented by this dimension include:

1. *Upper- and lower-case forms.* Knowledge that letters come in two analogous forms and that there are rules governing when the two forms are used.
2. *Letter names.* Knowledge of the names and corresponding written symbols for the 26 individual letters.
3. *Concept of letter.* Knowledge about the functions of letters.

Words

The four objectives specific to this domain include:

1. *Concept of word in print.* Knowledge that written words, as a distinct unit of print, correspond spoken words.
2. *Short words and long words.* Knowledge that written words are a distinct unit of print and are composed of letters.
3. *Letters and words.* Knowledge that written words are distinct from the other salient form of print (letters) and that words have meaning.
4. *Word identification.* Knowledge of some words in print, including one's own name and other high-frequency or high-function words.

SEQUENCE OF INSTRUCTION

In the preceding sections we described a fourfold scope of instruction along with 15 objectives that, if addressed in a *systematic* plan over time by calling attention to print during shared reading interactions, will result in substantial increases in children's knowledge about print (Justice et al., 2009). A systematic plan involves organizing and delivering instruction so that it follows an established pattern through which objectives are addressed. Systematic instruction requires sequentially organizing content so that what children learn accumulates in an orderly fashion over time. Instruction that follows an organized sequence provides educators with the opportunity to review and build upon previously learned concepts rather than proceeding haphazardly. The notion of systematic-ness has received considerable interest in the last decade as an important aspect of literacy instruction, as some evidence has suggested that *systematic* instruction in early reading instruction is an important mechanism for promoting children's growth in literacy programs (e.g., Foorman, Fletcher, Francis, Schatschneider, & Mehta, 1998).

There are numerous ways to sequence print-knowledge instruction, or any type of literacy instruction, for that matter, so that it proceeds in a systematic manner over time. The concept of systematic or sequenced instruction does not necessarily mean that one needs to follow a developmental course of instruction in which teaching proceeds linearly (and vertically) from easier to more difficult concepts. Rather, the concept need only imply that a *sequence* is being pursued, thereby allowing children's knowledge to accumulate in a systematic and sus-tained manner over time. Eventually, the logic of the system of rules that gov-erns print forms and functions will be incorporated by children (Adams, 2002).

Generally, systematic instruction follows one of three sequences to ensure that a specific scope of instruction and the objectives contained therein are cov-ered (Fey, 1986):

1. Vertical instruction.
2. Horizontal instruction.
3. Cyclical instruction.

Figure 3.2 provides an overview of what vertical instruction typically looks like. Here, we have organized the fourfold scope of print knowledge and its 15 objectives so that all objectives are addressed systematically over a 30-week period of instruction. As can be seen, with vertically sequenced instruction, a set of objectives is arranged in a linear sequence, and instruction targeting those objectives proceeds vertically over time (from the first objective to the last objec-tive). Typically, only one or two objectives are addressed at a given point in time; the intent is for the child to achieve mastery on a given objective before the next objective in a sequence is tackled. For the purposes of illustration, we developed a vertical progression of print-knowledge instruction so that we first address objectives within two dimensions of the scope (print and book organization, print meaning) early in the year and then build upon these with the other two dimensions within the scope (letters, words) (see Figure 3.2). If one adhered strictly to a vertical progression of instruction, one would not want to move from one objective (e.g., knowledge of title of book) to the next in a sequence (e.g., knowledge of author) until mastery of the first was demonstrated. Consistent

Instructional weeks	Book and print organization	Print meaning
Week 1	Title of book	Function of print
	Author of book	Environmental print
	Page order	
	Page organization	Concept of reading
	Print direction	
	Letters	**Words**
	Upper- and lower-case forms	Concept of word in print
		Short words and long words
	Letter names	Letters and words
		Word identification
Week 30	Concept of letter	Concept of word in print

FIGURE 3.2. Scope of print-knowledge instruction: Vertical sequence.

with assumptions inherent in vertical approaches to instruction, this sequence reflects the assumption that children must first develop basic knowledge about print (e.g., knowledge that the function of print generally is to convey meaning) upon which they will build more sophisticated understandings (e.g., knowledge that letters come in two analogous forms).

Ordering instruction to address a vertical sequencing of skills is somewhat typical in early literacy instruction. For instance, the popular classroom curriculum *Phonemic Awareness in Young Children* (Adams, Foorman, Lundberg, & Beeler, 1998) follows a vertical progression of skill development, in which objectives within a sevenfold scope of instruction are vertically organized along a linear pathway of phonological awareness development, beginning with objectives focused on developing general listening skills and culminating with objectives focused on recognizing relationships between letters and sounds. Instruction that follows a vertical progression of skill development can be effective in fostering children's skill acquisition in a variety of different developmental domains (e.g., Schuele et al., 2008). One of the major criticisms of vertical approaches is that they tend to deconstruct complex areas of development into a linear progression of isolated skills, yet often development does not proceed along linear and vertically arranged pathways (e.g., Anthony, Lonigan, Driscoll, Phillips, & Burgess, 2003). For instance, there is little evidence that children must have basic foundational knowledge about print functions before they can acquire more sophisticated understanding about the functions of letters; rather, some recent findings from developmental science suggest that development may not proceed in such a hierarchical manner (see Anthony et al., 2003). An additional criticism concerns the rate of instruction, particularly whether working on one or two objectives at a time until mastery is reached is the most efficient means to foster children's growth.

Figure 3.3 provides an alternative to vertical approaches of organizing instruction: a horizontal approach for sequencing objectives (Fey, 1986). Note that the primary difference between the horizontal and the vertical approaches is that the former presents the option of addressing multiple areas of development simultaneously, which, in our case, meant the entire fourfold scope of print-knowledge instruction: book and print organization, print meaning, letters, and words. Using this approach, children develop knowledge across four distinct (albeit interrelated) dimensions of print knowledge simultaneously. In Week 1, for instance, children would be taught beginning concepts about (1) the way in which books are organized (e.g., location of title and author), (2) the various functions served by print, (3) the difference between upper- and lower-case forms, and (4) the concept of word in print. The benefit of horizontal approaches is that they broaden what is taught from one or two focal areas to three or more; consequently, one is able to teach more at a single point in time and, presumably, be more efficient. Horizontal approaches are similar to vertical approaches in their objective that children achieve mastery of a specific unit of knowledge before tackling the next in a sequence.

Yet another option for organizing systematic instruction, aside from vertical and horizontal approaches, is a cyclical approach. This approach to instruction

Instructional weeks	Scope of Instruction			
	Book and print organization	Print meaning	Letters	Words
Week 1	Title of book	Function of print	Upper- and lower-case forms	Concept of word in print
	Author of book	Environmental print		Short words and long words
	Page order		Letter names	Letters and words
	Page organization	Concept of reading		Word identification
				Concept of word in print
Week 30	Print direction		Concept of letter	in print

FIGURE 3.3. Scope of print-knowledge instruction: Horizontal sequence.

largely emerged from treatment of children with significant speech–sound disorders (Hodson, 1989), which traditionally had relied upon vertical and horizontal approaches to ordering instruction focused on remediating problematic sounds. Similar to the vertical and horizontal approaches to sequencing instruction, a cyclical approach addresses all print-knowledge objectives in a systematic manner. The primary difference is that in the cyclical approach, one does not wait for mastery of a certain concept or objective. Rather, one moves on to the next objective in a sequence, but then continues to cycle back through objectives so that they are addressed repeatedly over time. Figure 3.4 provides an example of how a cyclical approach might be used to address the 15 print-knowledge objectives.

The benefit to a cyclical approach is that it exposes children to important objectives even if they have not mastered foundational knowledge or skills; this may be particularly relevant to children who are developing foundational

Instructional weeks	Scope of Instruction			
	Book and print organization	Print meaning	Letters	Words
Week 1	Print direction	Environmental print	Upper- and lower-case forms	Concept of word in print
	Author of book			
	Page organization	Concept of reading	Concept of letter	Word identification
	Title of book	Function of print	Letter names	Letters and words
	Page organization	Environmental print	Concept of letter	Word identification
	Author of book			
	Page order	Function of print	Upper- and lower-case forms	Letters and words
	Title of book	Concept of reading	Concept of letter	Short words and long words
	Page organization			
	Page order	Environmental print	Letter names	Word identification
	Print direction	Concept of reading	Upper- and lower-case forms	Letters and words
Week 30	Page order			

FIGURE 3.4. Scope of print-knowledge instruction: Cyclical sequence.

knowledge or skills quite slowly, but they may need to develop a large body of knowledge quite rapidly. For instance, consider the circumstances of 5-year-old Rashaun who has a significant disorder of language and is developing knowledge about print quite slowly. Because Rashaun will enter first grade and begin formal reading instruction in less than 1 year, it may be beneficial to expose him to all of our print-knowledge objectives in as short as possible a time. In addition, a cyclical approach may more readily approximate development than vertical and horizontal approaches, in that some evidence suggests that children's language and literacy development proceeds in "fits and starts" (e.g., speeds up and slows down) rather than in a clear linear trajectory (Pence & Justice, 2007).

In our work on calling attention to print, we have largely adhered to using a cyclical pattern in which print objectives are recycled over and over during a period of instruction. Figure 3.5 presents one example of our approach to sequencing objectives in a cyclical sequence of instruction that addresses 15 print-knowledge objectives over a 30-week period of instruction (which approximates an academic year in many preschool settings, giving or taking a few weeks of holiday breaks). These objectives can be systematically addressed in weekly reading routines during which teachers or other adults (literacy coaches, parents, speech–language pathologists) call attention to print.

In a recent study (Justice et al., 2009), preschool teachers addressed these objectives four times per week in large-group classroom-based reading sessions, and we compared growth in print knowledge for children in their classrooms compared to children in classrooms in which teachers used the same books along the same reading schedule, but did not systematically address any of the print objectives. We found that children whose teachers used this cyclical approach to organizing print-knowledge instruction made significantly greater gains on three measures of print knowledge (alphabet knowledge, print concepts knowledge, and name writing skill) compared to children in the comparison classrooms.

INTENSITY OF INSTRUCTION

Intensity refers to how often something takes place. With respect to instruction, intensity often refers to how often sessions occur (e.g., twice per week vs. four times per week), but it also can refer to how often one teaches something within a given session. To differentiate between the two uses of the term, we use *intensity* to refer to how often one reads books to children (during which the adult calls attention to print to address a scope and sequence of instruction) and the term *teaching episode* to refer to how often one teaches something within a given session.

Week	Print-knowledge objectives	
1	Environmental print	Concept of reading
2	Print direction	Concept of word in print
3	Author of book	Function of print
4	Upper- and lower-case forms	Page organization
5	Title of book	Word identification
6	Concept of letter	Page organization
7	Page order	Letter names
8	Word identification	Concept of letter
9	Author of book	Letters and words
10	Short words and long words	Function of print
11	Concept of letter	Environmental print
12	Upper- and lower-case forms	Page order
13	Title of book	Function of print
14	Page organization	Short words and long words
15	Letter names	Concept of reading
16	Concept of letter	Page order
17	Letters and words	Letter names
18	Upper- and lower-case forms	Concept of word in print
19	Short words and long words	Print direction
20	Page organization	Concept of reading
21	Word identification	Print direction
22	Title of book	Upper- and lower-case forms
23	Environmental print	Page order
24	Concept of print in word	Print direction
25	Letter names	Concept of reading
26	Letters and words	Function of print
27	Title of book	Word identification
28	Author of book	Environmental print
29	Short words and long words	Author of book
30	Concept of word in print	Letters and words

FIGURE 3.5. Cyclical approach to systematically addressing instructional objectives.

Generally, in our research on calling attention to print, we have found an intensity of about three to four reading sessions per week to be sufficient for accelerating children's knowledge about print (Justice & Ezell, 2000, 2002). Moreover, within each of these sessions, we generally recommend that adults embed about four *total* teaching episodes, or about one or two per objective being addressed, as we have also found that this is sufficient for significantly increasing children's knowledge about print in relatively short periods of time (e.g., Justice & Ezell, 2002; Justice et al., 2009). Offering any more attention to print than this within a book reading session might run the risk of detracting children's interest from other parts of a book that also warrant their attention.

Figure 3.6 shows the cumulative amount of attention each objective addressed within Week 1 (following the sequence of instruction presented in Figure 3.5) would receive if we adhered to this suggestion regarding overall intensity and number of teaching episodes. Specifically, within 1 week of instruction featuring four reading sessions (occurring on four different days), which we assume last about 10–15 minutes per session, the two objectives (i.e., environmental print, concept of reading) addressed during the week would each be discussed between four and eight times. The observation sheet presented in Figure 3.7 offers one tool for examining the number of teaching episodes embedded within a reading session. The tool can be used to provide a general metric of one's attention to the variety of print-knowledge objectives that can be addressed when reading with children, or it can be used as a tool for monitoring one's fidelity to the objectives as organized within a scope and sequence of instruction (see Figure 3.5).

As evidence to the point that we need not provide any more attention to print concepts to accelerate children's learning, Figure 3.8 provides a comparison of alphabet knowledge growth over a 2-month period for 15 children who experienced three references to letters within thrice-weekly small-group reading

Week	Day	Book title	Objectives	Teaching episodes
1	1	*My First Day of School*	Environmental print Concept of reading	1–2 1–2
	2	*My First Day of School*	Environmental print Concept of reading	1–2 1–2
	3	*My First Day of School*	Environmental print Concept of reading	1–2 1–2
	4	*My First Day of School*	Environmental print Concept of reading	1–2 1–2

FIGURE 3.6. Intensity and instructional episodes in 1 week of calling attention to print.

Reader: _____ Text: _____

Observer: _____ Date: _____

Too little = Topics/targets not addressed, opportunities missed
Just right = Topics/targets addressed at just the right amount
Too much = Topics/targets addressed at level that seemed too high, seemed to detract from session

Scale	Description	Too little	Just right	Too much	Comments
Book and Print Organization	Title of book Author of book Page order Page organization Print direction				
Print Meaning	Function of print Environmental print Concept of reading				
Letters	Upper- and lower-case forms Letter names Concept of letter				
Words	Concept of words in print Short words and long words Letters and words Word identification				

FIGURE 3.7. Calling Attention to Print Observation.

From *Engaging Children with Print* by Laura M. Justice and Amy E. Sofka. Copyright 2010 by The Guilford Press. Permission to photocopy this figure is granted to purchasers of this book for personal use only (see copyright page for details).

62

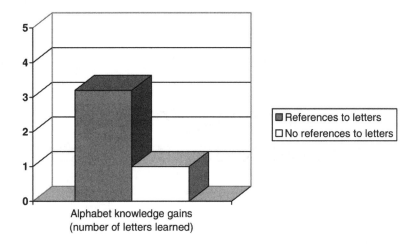

FIGURE 3.8. Alphabet knowledge gains for preschool-age children with three references to letters embedded into thrice-weekly reading sessions over a 2-month period. Adapted from Justice and Ezell (2002). Copyright 2002 by the American Speech–Language–Hearing Association. Adapted by permission.

sessions, as compared to 15 children who were read the same books on the same schedule, but without these teaching episodes embedded into their reading sessions. As the data in this figure show, calling attention to print need not dominate reading interactions to propel children's learning forward. We emphasize that one's goal is to elevate print status so that it be an important part of the book in the eye of the child, but that it need not dominate. Other features of the book, including illustrations, concepts, and characters, are worthy of conversation as well.

CHAPTER 4

Matching Books
with Print-Knowledge Targets

As we have discussed in previous chapters, several studies have shown that children, in general, do not attend to or ask questions about print without prompting by an adult or knowledgeable other (e.g., Justice et al., 2009). However, once print is elevated to a rightful subject for conversation, children become interested and engaged in discussing such features of print as specific names of letters, interesting written words, print direction, and environmental print. We have thus far emphasized the important role that adult readers—such as preschool teachers and parents—can play in elevating children's interest in and engagement with print.

Yet, the books one reads with children when calling attention to print are anything but a trivial matter. Rather, the books shared with children, when one's goal is to stimulate their attention to and learning about print, need to exhibit features of print worth talking about. We refer to this variety of books—a heterogeneous lot, at that—as *print-salient books.* These are books in which print is an interesting or even remarkable design characteristic. Studies of references to print during storybook reading show that the amount of print-focused discussion is higher when teachers read books containing relatively high amounts of print-salient features (Smolkin, Conlon, & Yaden, 1988; Zucker et al., 2009). This should come as no surprise since, for instance, having a focused discussion about the difference between upper- and lower-case letter forms is made much easier for the adult and child when the print being examined is in a very large font and features distinct differences between the forms, such as a color change from the upper-case to the lower-case letters.

IDENTIFYING PRINT-SALIENT TEXTS

Many, but by no means all, children's texts feature interesting and discussion-worthy characteristics that bring print to the potential forefront of the child's attention. Some of the more common characteristics include these (Smolkin et al., 1988; Zucker et al., 2009):

1. *Labels.* Items depicted in illustrations are labeled with their names or other relevant information (e.g., the word *owl* appears next to a picture of an owl).

2. *Environmental print.* Authentic representations of print are depicted in illustrations (e.g., an illustration of a school bus includes the word *school bus* along its side).

3. *Visible sound.* Sounds are spelled out (e.g., *purrrrr* appears next to a picture of a cat).

4. *Visible speech and speech bubbles.* Words produced by characters are presented in bubbles placed near their heads.

5. *Letters in isolation.* Alphabet letters appear in isolation from other text.

6. *Typesetting changes.* Changes to text that affect type style, font, and type size, orientation, and/or color, such as type that gets larger to represent a loud word or type that moves up and down to represent waves in an ocean.

Texts that contain a large number of these features do seem to stimulate more conversation about print when adults and children read books together compared to texts with few of these features. Zucker and colleagues (2009) studied verbal references to print for 17 preschool teachers when reading six different texts in their classrooms as a large-group activity. These researchers coded each of the six texts for the number of print-salient features contained on each page, using a tool they termed the print salience metric (PSM). Specifically, a PSM score was calculated for each page of text that represented the total instances of print in illustrations (i.e., labels, environmental print, visible sound, visible speech, letters in isolation) and total instances of typesetting changes in the body of the text (e.g., change of type style, change of formatting, change of size, change of orientation, change of type color); this number was then divided by the number of pages within a given text to control for variations in the length of different books. Three texts the teachers read had high PSM scores, averaging

3.81 per page of text, whereas three texts had low PSM scores, averaging 0.44 per page of text. The researchers coded teachers' verbal references to print across the four dimensions of print knowledge (book and print organization, print meaning, letters, words) for the two sets of books, as presented in Figure 4.1. As the data show, when teachers read books with a relatively high number of print-salient features, they talked about print about twice as much as they did when reading books with relatively fewer instances of print-salient features. This study suggests that the texts one selects to read with children can play an important role in providing interesting opportunities to talk about print within the text.

The PSM can be readily and reliably applied to any children's text; it appears in Figure 4.2. Developed by Zucker and colleagues (2009), the PSM captures two categories of print-salient features that may occur in children's texts: *print in illustrations* and *type changes in body of text.* The first category includes four mutually exclusive items to look for in a text: labels, environmental print, visible sound, and visible speech. Labels are often found in informational texts and usually occur with illustrations, graphs, figures, and/or photographs. Environmental print is typically embedded within illustrations, such as "Stop" on a stop sign, "Carson" on a child's cubby at school, or "Enter" written over a doorway (numbers are not included in this category). Visible sound occurs when sounds are spelled out in print, such as "grrrr" from a tiger's mouth, "whhrrrr" from the engine of a plane, or "crunch, crunch, crunch" from a caterpillar's mouth. Visible speech is marked by words or speech bubbles present near a character indicating that he or she is talking, as in the word "Hello!" depicted near a butterfly.

The second category, type changes in body of text, includes five nonmutually exclusive items: changes in font, formatting, type size, orientation, and color. A

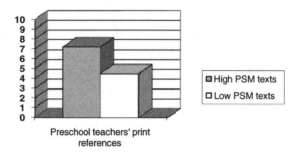

FIGURE 4.1. Differences in preschool teachers' print references when reading books with a large number of print-salient features (high-PSM texts) and a low number of print-salient features (low-PSM texts). Adapted from Zucker, Justice, and Piasta (2009). Copyright by the American Speech–Language–Hearing Association. Adapted by permission.

Step 1	Calculate total story pages	Determine total number of pages containing text and/or story illustrations. Exclude the front matter of the text (i.e., end pages, title page, copyright, dedication page) and end pages or copyright pages at the end of the text.
Step 2	Count the number of instances print is embedded in illustrations	Tally each instance of print embedded in illustrations based on these categories. These four categories are mutually exclusive, in that one instance of print can only be coded in one category: • *Labels*: Count each label within illustrations, figures, or photographs. Labels often occur with diagrams in informational texts. • *Environmental Print:* Count each instance of environmental print. This is any time an object depicted in the illustration has a label, word, or letter on it. Environmental print often occurs on everyday objects, such as a box labeled "Toys" or a bus labeled "School Bus." Numerals should not be considered. • *Visible Sound:* Count each instance of sound in illustrations, such as when a character or object has a sound written nearby. For example, a snake with *sss* near its mouth or a television remote with "Click" beside it are instances of visible sound. • *Visible Speech:* Count each instance of speech in illustrations, such as when a character has words or speech balloons nearby indicating he or she is speaking.
Step 3	Count the number of type changes represented in body of text	Tally each instance of a change in type in the body or narrative of the text. These codes are not mutually exclusive, whereby one type change might be represented by several codes (e.g., type changes in both color and size). A change must occur within a two-page spread. • *Change of Type Style:* Count each instance when a new typesetting or font is used (e.g., changing the type from a block style to a serif style). • *Change of Formatting:* Count each instance when the formatting has been altered from a normal/regular font to bold, italics, underline, or all capitalized letters. • *Change of Type Size:* Count each change of type size (e.g., type is made larger). • *Change of Orientation:* Count each instance when the orientation of the text is changed. For example, a change from standard, horizontal text to setting the text at an angle is a change of orientation. • *Change of Type Color:* Count each instance when the type is printed in a different color. For example, the type is changed from a standard black to red for a word/letter.
Step 4	Calculate average print-salient elements per page of text	Calculate the sum of all print in illustrations and type changes codes. Divide by the total number of book pages to obtain the print salience metric score, which represents the average number of print-salient elements per page.

FIGURE 4.2. Print Salience Metric (PSM) coding procedures. From Zucker, Justice, and Piasta (2009). Copyright by the American Speech–Language–Hearing Association. Adapted by permission.

change in type style, for instance, occurs when the type shifts from **block** to **comic sans**. Formatting changes occur when type goes from regular font to **bold**, *italics,* ALL CAPITAL LETTERS, or <u>underlining</u>. A change in type size and color are just that—the type is made larger and/or the color changes from black to yellow for a word or letter. A change of orientation occurs when text moves from a horizontal setting to a slant or slope on the page. It can be enjoyable to collect a stack of children's texts and analyze them for the presence of interesting print features; some books will contain very few instances of print-salient features, whereas in other texts, these features will be abundant.

For the reader's reference, Appendix A presents PSM scores for 100 selected children's texts, 30 of which were previously presented in Chapter 3 as aligned with the scope and sequence of a 30-week reading program (see Figure 3.5). As you examine these PSM scores, it is important to note that the number of print-salient features by page is quite variable across texts. For instance, *The Scrambled States of America Talent Show* and *Superhero ABC* both have PSM scores higher than 9, mainly because each has a large quantity of environmental print embedded within the illustrations along with a number of type changes in color, size, and orientation. On the other hand, *A Color of His Own* and *The Mitten* have PSM scores of 0, indicating that these texts have virtually no remarkable print features.

MATCHING TEXTS WITH PRINT-KNOWLEDGE OBJECTIVES

Not all children's texts are ideal for targeting specific print-knowledge objectives, such as environmental print (an objective under the print meaning dimension), by calling attention to print when reading with children. This target is best addressed when sharing a text that has instances of environmental print embedded within the illustration. Other targets, however, are not as sensitive to a high level of print saliency. For instance, conversations surrounding page organization and the concept of reading can occur regardless of the presence of labels, speech bubbles, environmental print, or visible sound or speech within a text. To address specific objectives within the four dimensions of print knowledge (book and print organization, print meaning, letters, and words), it can be helpful to link specific books that exemplify particular print features to particular objectives. For instance, the text *Miss Bindergarten Goes to Kindergarten* would be an ideal choice for discussing the differences between letters and words (an objective within the dimension of words), because it includes print-salient features that make letters and words highly visible in the text design; on the other hand, *A Color of His Own* would be an appropriate choice for discussing page organization (an objective within the dimension of print and book organization), as it would be quite simple to embed a discussion about how one reads a story from the top to bottom of a page using this book.

The systematic approach to print-knowledge instruction presented in Figure 4.3 features a different text being read each week, with two different print targets highlighted during that week. For instance, during the first week of reading (*My First Day of School*), environmental print and the concept of reading are addressed. During the second week of reading (*There's a Dragon at My School*), print direction and the concept of the word in print are addressed. Following this cyclical pattern, each of 15 targets is focused on repeatedly over time in a systematic sequence of instruction, leading to significant increases in children's knowledge about print.

Cards placed within each text can be used to offer a reminder to adult readers of the specific objectives being addressed, as well as to provide a particularly

Week	Book Title	Print-Knowledge Objectives
1	*My First Day of School*	Environmental print Concept of reading
2	*There's a Dragon at My School*	Print direction Concept of words in print
3	*I Like it When . . .*	Author of book Function of print
4	*The Dandelion Seed*	Upper- and lower-case forms Page organization
5	*Down by the Cool of the Pool*	Title of book Word identification
6	*"More More More," Said the Baby*	Concept of letter Page organization
7	*Jamboree Day*	Page order Letter names
8	*Rumble in the Jungle*	Word identification Concept of letter
9	*David Gets in Trouble*	Author of book Letters and words
10	*The Way I Feel*	Short words and long words Function of print
11	*Spot Bakes a Cake*	Concept of letter Environmental print *(cont.)*

FIGURE 4.3. Books linked with specific print-knowledge objectives.

Week	Book Title	Print-Knowledge Objectives
12	We're Going on a Bear Hunt	Upper- and lower-case forms Page order
13	Dear Mr. Blueberry	Title of book Function of print
14	Growing Vegetable Soup	Page organization Short words and long words
15	Froggy Gets Dressed	Letter names Concept of reading
16	I Stink!	Concept of letter Page order
17	Animal Action ABC	Letters and words Letter names
18	My Backpack	Upper- and lower-case forms Concept of word in print
19	Baghead	Short words and long words Print direction
20	A Color of His Own	Page organization Concept of reading
21	To Market, to Market	Word identification Print direction
22	Hey, Little Ant	Title of book Upper- and lower-case forms
23	Mouse Mess	Environmental print Page order
24	In the Small, Small Pond	Concept of words in print Print direction
25	The Grumpy Morning	Letter names Concept of reading
26	The Noisy Airplane Ride	Letters and words Function of print
27	How to Speak Moo!	Title of book Word identification
28	Never Spit on Your Shoes	Author of book Environmental print
29	The Recess Queen	Short words and long words Author of book
30	Miss Bindergarten Gets Ready for Kindergarten	Concept of word in print Letters and words

FIGURE 4.3 (cont.)

helpful means for promoting the systematicness of this approach. Figure 4.4 contains an example of a card—to which we refer to as a "STAR card" (Sit Together and Read)—that we developed to provide a reminder of the print objectives to be discussed when reading *My First Day of School* (environmental print, concept of reading); these cards provide explicit guidance on how specific objectives might be addressed, with suggested language to use. For instance, to address the target of environmental print, the adult reader might say, "We see letters and words at the bottom of this page. Who can show me where we see letters and words somewhere else?" Here the adult reader is attempting to elicit children's awareness of environmental print embedded within a particular illustration, including logos printed on the side of a bread bag and a cereal box. Figure 4.5 provides a blank card that can be used to develop a STAR card for any text; one can use this as

---

My First Day of School

TARGET: Environmental Print

Teacher: We see words and letters at the bottom of this page. Who can show me where we see words and letters somewhere else?

Child: Here? (*Points to tray of food.*)

Teacher: Almost. Here are some letters and words on the cereal box. (*Reads "Snappy Snax," then moves to calendar and bread bag.*)

TARGET: Concept of Reading

Teacher: This book is called *My First Day of School.* I can't wait to read this book. I think we are going to learn about being at school on the first day, and maybe about meeting new friends, too. What else are we going to learn?

Child: Look at the pictures of the boy!

Teacher: We will look at pictures of the boy, and we're going to *read* it, and learn all kinds of things about school and being there on the first day . . .

STAR: Sit Together and Read

FIGURE 4.4. STAR card for print objectives when reading *My First Day at School*

Book Title:

TARGET:

Notes:

TARGET:

Notes:

STAR: Sit Together and Read

FIGURE 4.5. Blank card for developing a STAR card for any text.

a tool to develop written prompts or notes for oneself regarding how to address certain objectives, jotted down in advance of a reading session.

Appendix B identifies the scope and sequence of storybooks for a 30-week reading program and offers a tracking sheet for print-knowledge objectives. Appendix C provides all of the STAR cards that were developed to help adult readers address the fourfold scope and sequence of 15 print-knowledge objectives during a 30-week period of systematic instruction, using a set of 30 commercially available children's texts. Readers will note that the STAR cards also provide guidance on how to support children's participation in print-focused reading sessions using high- and low-support strategies; we discuss these strategies in depth in Chapter 5. In the remainder of this chapter we provide a thorough accounting of the cyclical objectives as linked to and addressed within the 30 texts, as well as a sample dialogue that might occur when discussing the various print targets with children. The scope and sequence call for highlighting only two print concepts at a time per book, but, as additional concepts are introduced, the books can be recycled to accommodate other suitable targets.

WEEK 1

Book: *My First Day of School*

Targets: Environmental print; concept of reading

Target Definition

- *Environmental print.* Knowledge about the specific and varying functions served by print within the environment, such as on signs, logos, and posters.

- *Concept of reading.* Knowledge of the purposes of reading, such as to gain information and for enjoyment, and that reading is an act in which people engage.

Book Features

My First Day of School, by P. K. Hallinan (1987), is ideally suited for highlighting both environmental print as well as concept of reading. As the title implies, it is a child's first day of school. From getting ready in the morning, to walking to school, to arriving in his classroom, the illustrations depicting our new student are rich with examples of *environmental print.* From the cereal box, calendar, and bread bag in the kitchen, to the name tags, cubbies, safety patrol, and bulletin board, this book provides plenty of opportunity to intersperse story reading with questions about print.

Sample Dialogue

ADULT: I see words in some different places on this page, like right here on this cereal box. Can you show me where there is another word in an unusual place on this page?

CHILD: (*Points to illustration.*)

ADULT: Not quite—here is another word in an unusual place on the page. (*Points to "Safety First" sign on the wall.*)

From the very first reading of this highly descriptive title, an adult can begin to converse about the *purpose of reading* in terms of a very real event in a child's life. Every young child is curious about school. Questions such as "What will school be like?", "Will I make friends?", and "Can I still play games?" can be discussed in terms of the book's character: a little boy experiencing school for the first time. If a child is already in school and this book is read, comparisons can be made across their school days. A child may learn that his or her day is much like the lead character's, or the child may find out that a typical school day may be very different for other children.

Sample Dialogue

ADULT: This boy is a little nervous about his first day of school. Do you remember your first day? What were some of the things you were worried about?

CHILD: I was afraid I would get lost and not be able to find my classroom.

ADULT: How can we find out if this little boy is worried about the same things you were?

CHILD: We have to read the book and find out.

ADULT: Exactly right. We are going to read and find out information about this little boy's first day of school.

WEEK 2

Book: There's a Dragon at My School

Targets: Print direction; concept of word in print

Target Definition

- *Print direction.* Knowledge of how print moves from left to right.

- *Concept of words in print.* Knowledge that written words, as a distinct unit of print, correspond to spoken words.

Book Features

There's a Dragon at My School, by Jenny Tyler and Philip Hawthorn (1996), is a story about a child who brings a pet dragon to school. As can be imagined, havoc ensues as the dragon "breaks every rule." Finding print on the page and discussing *print direction* becomes a predictable task with this text since all the obvious print is found at the top of the left-hand page, and runs directly left to right. This format makes highlighting print direction quite straightforward.

Sample Dialogue

ADULT: Here are the words on the page. Which way do I need to read the words? Can you show me?

CHILD: (*Runs finger along the text from left to right.*)

ADULT: Yes, you got it! We read words from left to right.

While the *concept of word in print* can certainly be discussed using the main story text, an additional feature of this book is that it utilizes flaps on the right-hand pages to delight and surprise a young audience. On one page the word *plunk* is found after lifting up the piano lid flap; the dragon has dumped sand inside it. Having one word displayed in this way throughout the book makes teaching the concept of the word in print an easily explicit task.

Sample Dialogue

ADULT: This book has a lot of words hidden under the flaps. Let's lift this one and see if we find another word. Oh, look! This word says *Yum*. I see it again— *Yum*. Let's lift the next flap. Can you point to the word we find under it?

CHILD: Look, here it is! What does it say? He did something to the bathroom!

ADULT: He sure did, and someone isn't going to be happy! You are right, that is the word, and it says *Glug*.

WEEK 3

Book: *I Like It When …*

Targets: Author of book; function of print

Target Definition

- *Author of book.* Knowledge of what an author is and where the name of the author is located in a book (on the cover and on the title page, typically); this category also includes children's knowledge of the role of the illustrator.

- *Function of print.* Knowledge that the function of print generally is to convey meaning.

Book Features

I Like It When ..., by Mary Murphy (1997), describes many things a young penguin likes to do with his loved one. The *author's name* is very clearly present in block type on the front of the book under the title; this is the only text on the cover. This makes the task of finding the author's name quite explicit, without potential distractions such as inclusion of the word *by.*

Sample Dialogue

ADULT: We can usually find the author's name on the front of the book. Here it is—her name is Mary Murphy. Point to the author's name for me.

CHILD: (*Points to author's name.*)

ADULT: We talked about what the author does. Tell me again what the author does.

CHILD: The author writes the words to the story.

ADULT: You are right. Mary Murphy wrote the words to our story *I Like It When....*

Each page of this story has a different activity, such as reading stories, dancing, and taking a bath, along with descriptive text and illustrations. These activities all occur as things "I like...." Discussion can center on the fact that the print in the story describes what makes the small penguin happy; the *print's function* is to convey this happiness and what makes it occur.

Sample Dialogue

ADULT: This little penguin loves to do different things. The words in the story tell us what these different things are. He likes to play peekaboo and to be tickled. Look here, it says he likes dancing. Do the words help us understand what the penguin enjoys doing?

CHILD: Yes, and he likes to read stories too, but I don't like to take a bath.

ADULT: I know you don't like to take a bath. The words in your own story would not say that you liked to do that!

WEEK 4

Book: *The Dandelion Seed*

Targets: Upper- and lower-case forms; page organization

Target Definition

- *Upper- and lower-case forms.* Knowledge that letters come in two analogous forms and that there are rules governing when the two forms are used.

- *Page organization.* Knowledge of how a page with multiple lines of text is read from top to bottom.

Book Features

The Dandelion Seed, by Joseph Anthony (1997), tells the tale of a dandelion seed's seasonal journey to becoming a flower with its very own seeds. The first sentence of each page is punctuated with a large, bold *upper-case letter,* making pointing this out, or having the child find it, an explicit, rewarding task, since this letter form is so distinguishable from the lower-case form.

Sample Dialogue

ADULT: This is an upper-case letter *T,* this is an upper-case letter *D,* and this is an upper-case letter *S.* Can you point to another upper-case letter on the cover of this book?

CHILD: (*Points to the lower-case* h *in* The)

ADULT: Not quite. That is a lower-case *h.* Here, here is another upper-case letter, *J,* in the author's name. That was a tricky question!

As noted in the definition, *page organization* deals with the knowledge that lines of print are read from top to bottom. This story makes use of multiple lines of text throughout, providing the reader with many opportunities to call attention to this target. An additional fun feature of this book, however, is that the lines of text may be found not only in the middle of the page, but also at the top or bottom of the page. This may complicate the task a bit, since children will need to locate the actual print, but once found, the concept of reading multiple lines of text top to bottom is reinforced, no matter where print occurs on the page.

Sample Dialogue

ADULT: There are two lines of print on this page. Which line do I read first?

CHILD: (*Points to the first line of text.*)

ADULT: I knew you would remember that. Yes, that is right, we read this line first, and we read this line last.

WEEK 5

Book: *Down by the Cool of the Pool*

Targets: Title of book; word identification

Target Definition

- *Title of book.* Knowledge of where the title is located in a book (on the cover and on the title page, typically) and what the function of the title is.

- *Word identification.* Knowledge of some words in print, including one's own name and other high-frequency or high-function words.

Book Features

Down by the Cool of the Pool, by Tony Mitton (2001), is a story of animals showing one another how they can dance in different ways. Eventually, they all topple into a pool, but continue their dancing until the sun goes down. The *title* is clearly represented at the top of the page, in relatively large type, with an illustration of a pool directly below it. The representation of the pool makes guessing what the title says, and what the book is about, a fun, explicit task.

Sample Dialogue

ADULT: Here is the title of our book, right here. Show me where the title is.

CHILD: (*Points to the title.*)

ADULT: Thank you. Very good. The title of the book is right here. What do you think it says?

CHILD: The animals are swimming!

ADULT: Very good. The title is *Down by the Cool of the Pool.* I think you might be right, we might see animals swimming in the pool.

The repetition of the phrase "down by the cool of the pool," provides a perfect opportunity for the adult to help the child identify certain words in the story; this is defined as *word identification.* As children become familiar with the cadence of the story and the phrase "down by the cool of the pool," the adult can encourage choral reading when coming to this part of the story. By tracking each word while reading, the adult can emphasize each distinct word in the text.

Sample Dialogue

ADULT: Let's say these words together again and point to them as we say them … "down by the cool of the pool" (*adult and child together*). Very good. Point to the word that says *pool*.

CHILD: Here it is, this is the word *pool.*

ADULT: Wonderful. That is the word *pool.* Let's point to it each time we read it, OK?

WEEK 6

Book: *"More More More," Said the Baby*

Targets: Concept of letter; page organization

Target Definition

- *Concept of letter.* Knowledge about the functions of letters; that letters are units of print that correspond to sounds and are organized to build words.

- *Page organization.* Knowledge of how a page with multiple lines of text is read from top to bottom.

Book Features

"More More More," Said the Baby, by Vera B. Williams (1990), contains three vignettes of the joy and love babies evoke in those who care for them. Each vignette has its own title on a page without additional text. The uniform block letters make highlighting each letter within the word a clear-cut task. Without an overabundance of text, the *concept of letter* can be taught using just two words on each vignette's title page.

Sample Dialogue

ADULT: Wow, look at all the letter *M*'s in the title of our book. Here is one, and here is one (*pointing to first two* M's). And they all help make the word *More.* Point to the next letter *M* for me.

CHILD: *M* is right here. Look, more letters are the same.

ADULT: Yes, that is another letter *M* in the word *More,* just like the other *M*'s. I like how you noticed other letters that are the same. Show me which letters are the same.

CHILD: This one and this one and this one (*pointing to the letter* o *in each word* More).

ADULT: Good job! That is the letter *o,* and it helps the letter *M* make the word *More.*

The pages of this story are filled with beautiful illustrations of the babies and their caregivers. Lines of text are found at the top and/or bottom of each illustration. This format makes identifying *page organization* an engaging activity for the child, since not only must you read the lines at the top of the page from top to bottom, but you must also read the lines at the bottom of the page from top to bottom, having the break of the illustration between. This fact further highlights page organization on a macro level.

Sample Dialogue

ADULT: We're going to start reading at the top of the page, up here. There are more words down here, too. We'll read those, too. But we need to start up here. Where do I start to read, up here or down here?

CHILD: Up here.

ADULT: You are right. We'll start up here with this line and then go down here to finish reading the page.

WEEK 7

Book: *Jamboree Day*

Targets: Page order; letter names

Target Definition

- *Page order.* Knowledge of how books are read from front to back and that pages are read from left to right in a two-page spread.

- *Letter names.* Knowledge of the names and corresponding written symbols for the 26 individual letters.

Book Features

Jamboree Day, by Rhonda Gowler Greene (2001), follows the antics of jungle creatures who celebrate Jamboree Day together every May. Discussing *page order* is made fun and somewhat challenging in this book, since text alternates from being on the left-hand page to the right-hand page, until the very end, when text appears on both pages. When asking a child where you begin to read, he or she might point to the left page automatically, not noticing the lack of print. This can stimulate rich discussion of page order, and reading left to right, while also noticing that print must be present on the page in order for it to be read.

Sample Dialogue

ADULT: Oh, look! More animals are coming to the party. Let's keep reading. Which page should I read first? This one or this one?

CHILD: This one (*pointing to left page without text*).

ADULT: That was a hard question. We do start to read on the left page in a lot of books, but don't forget to look for the words. There aren't any words on the left page this time. They fooled us! The words start over here on this page, so that is where we need to start reading.

Pointing out individual letters using the names of the jungle animals is a useful, supportive way to target *letter names*. The *G* in *GIRAFFE*, the *Z* in *ZEBRA*, the *L* in *LION*, and the *F* in *FROG* can all be used to either introduce or reinforce individual letter names.

Sample Dialogue

ADULT: It looks like the zebra is coming to the party too. Who can remember what letter the word *zebra* starts with? We see it right here. Zachary, I bet you can remember this one.

CHILD: *Z*! It's in my name!

ADULT: I thought you might know that one, Zachary. A *Z* in *Zachary* and a *Z* in *ZEBRA*. It's right here.

WEEK 8

Book: *Rumble in the Jungle*

Targets: Word identification; concept of letter

Target Definition

- *Word identification.* Knowledge of some words in print, including one's own name and other high-frequency or high-function words.

- *Concept of letter.* Knowledge about the functions of letters; that letters are units of print that correspond to sounds and are organized to build words.

Book Features

Rumble in the Jungle, by Giles Andreae and David Wojtwoycz (1996), contains short, humorous rhymes about various jungle animals. With each animal's name highlighted prior to the text, targeting *word identification* is particularly easy to accomplish, especially since children can use the support of pictures to help them identify the words.

Sample Dialogue

ADULT: Oh, look at this animal. Who can tell me what this word says?

CHILDREN: *Tiger!*

ADULT: Exactly right, it says *tiger.* You remembered that from the last time we read it. And he looks like he is going to prowl around the jungle, doesn't he?

Again, when targeting the *concept of letter,* the animal names are quite useful. The print for each is in a clear, plain type, and each name stands alone in bold above the rest of the text. This makes it easy to track each letter while showing how these letters make up one word, as in *crocodile, hippopotamus,* and *gorilla.*

Sample Dialogue

ADULT: This word says *hippopotamus.* Let's all say it together … *hippopotamus.* Very good. I see three of the same letters that all help make the word *hippopotamus.*

CHILDREN: (*call out* p *and* o.)

ADULT: Oh, my! You all have good eyes. Look, here is the letter *o* and here is the letter *p.* There are more than one of each in the word *hippopotamus.* I think that we should count to see which letter shows up three times. Let's count the *o*'s first.

CHILDREN: (*Count to 2 with the adult.*)

ADULT: OK, so we have two *o*'s. Now let's count the letter *p*.

CHILDREN: (*Count to 3 with the adult.*)

ADULT: We have three *p*'s. So, which letter is in the word *hippopotamus* three times?

CHILDREN: (*Call out* p.)

ADULT: Yes! The letter *p* is in *hippopotamus* a lot! And how many times do we see the letter *o*?

CHILDREN: Two!

ADULT: Excellent. Let's keep reading.

WEEK 9

Book: *David Gets in Trouble*

Targets: Author of book; letters and words

Target Definition

- *Author of book.* Knowledge of what an author is and where the name of the author is located in a book (on the cover and on the title page, typically); this category also includes children's knowledge of the role of the illustrator.

- *Letters and words.* Knowledge that written words are distinct from the other salient form of print (letters) and that words have meaning.

Book Features

David Gets in Trouble, by David Shannon (2002), is a title that tells it all. Not only does our character David get in trouble, he won't admit he did anything wrong! When talking about the *role of author,* it is fun to have the children notice that the title of the book has the same name in it that the author's name does. Since our print-knowledge target, author of book, also includes the role of illustrator, the adult can also point out and discuss the fact that David Shannon not only wrote the book, but he illustrated it, too. This adds some complexity to the idea that "authors write the words, while illustrators draw the pictures." Sometimes, the author is both the author and the illustrator.

Sample Dialogue

ADULT: We are going to read the book titled *David Gets in Trouble*. It was written by a man named David Shannon. Who can tell me again what the author does?

CHILDREN: Writes the words!

ADULT: That is exactly right. And what does the illustrator do?

CHILDREN: Writes the pictures!

ADULT: Almost. The illustrator *draws* the pictures and the author writes the words. Let's read our story.

With sparse text and large, clear font, this story is well suited to encouraging children to notice *written words,* that *words* are *distinct* from *letters* (letters make up a word), and the context of the story promotes a conversation about the meaning of words. David is usually making up excuses for his accidents, and it is amusing to read and talk about all of David's "reasons" for something being broken, eaten, or forgotten. At the end of the book, David finally says "I'm sorry," which can also provoke a nuanced discussion of what those words mean in both the context of the story and real life.

Sample Dialogue

ADULT: David keeps getting into trouble, doesn't he? Look at him here. He is eating dog treats. Yuck! These words say *I was hungry!* That is David's reason for eating the treats. This is the word *hungry.* Daryl, come on up here and show me where the word *hungry* is.

CHILD: (*Points to* hungry.)

ADULT: What does that word say?

CHILD: That David is hungry.

ADULT: Yes, the word says *hungry,* and that is the excuse David is giving for eating dog treats.

WEEK 10

Book: *The Way I Feel*

Targets: Short words and long words; function of print

Target Definition

- *Short words and long words.* Knowledge that written words are a distinct unit of print composed of letters (some with many letters and others with few letters).

- *Function of print.* Knowledge that the function of print generally is to convey meaning.

Book Features

The Way I Feel, written and illustrated by Janan Cain (2000), describes all the ways in which how we feel may make us act, as well as various reasons we may feel certain emotions. The larger, colorfully represented emotion words provide an excellent opportunity to compare *short words and long words,* especially between that of *sad* and other words such as *scared* or *excited.*

Sample Dialogue

ADULT: Sad is a short word. It only has three letters in it. But look at the word *excited.* Let's count the number of letters in *excited.* (*Adult and children begin counting together.*) Seven letters in *excited,* but only three in *sad.* Is *sad* a short word or a long word?

CHILD: Short word!

ADULT: Yes, compared to the seven-letter word *excited, sad* is a short word with only three letters in it.

Highlighting the *function of print* is engaging with *The Way I Feel.* Each emotion word is written to evoke the emotion it represents. Thus, the word *scared* is written in a shaky font, whereas *angry* is thick, dark, and sharp. *Excited, on the other hand, is made up of bright colors with swirls and lines connoting bouncing. A conversation of these print features and the meaning they convey is a natural focus while reading this story.*

Sample Dialogue

ADULT: This is the word *scared.* Look at how it is written. It looks like it says *scared,* doesn't it? It is all shaky. Do you shake a little when you are scared?

CHILD: I shake like this (*imitating shaking*).

ADULT: See, you are shaking just like these letters in the word *scared* look like they are shaking. Now let's look at this word again. Hmmm, look at all the sharp points on the letters in this word. What do you think this word is?

CHILD: It looks mean, like it has teeth.

ADULT: That is so interesting. Those points do look like teeth, don't they? How might someone feel if they feel mean?

CHILD: Mad?

ADULT: You are right. And another word for *mad* is *angry,* and that is just what this word says, *angry.* The way it is written gives us a clue as to what the word says. What is this word again?

CHILD: *Angry!*

ADULT: Yes, *angry.* This little child is feeling angry. Let's find out why.

WEEK 11

Book: *Spot Bakes a Cake*

Targets: Concept of letter; function of print

Target Definition

- *Concept of letter.* Knowledge about the functions of letters; that letters are units of print that correspond to sounds and are organized to build words.

- *Function of print.* Knowledge that the function of print generally is to convey meaning.

Book Features

Spot Bakes a Cake, by Eric Hill (1994), is a familiar book to many and loved by children. The bold, block-type font makes calling attention to the *concept of letter* quite a clear-cut task. In particular, pointing out the letter *k* and its function in building the different words *bake, cake,* and *make* is easy, since readers follow Spot on his mission to bake a cake for his father's birthday.

Sample Dialogue

ADULT: We have looked at the letter *k* in our book *Spot Bakes a Cake* for a while now. Let's think of all the words the letter *k* helps to make. Jill, you go first.

Can you think of one word in our book that the letter *k* makes? We'll find it after you tell us.

CHILD: *Bake!* Spot is baking his daddy a cake.

ADULT: Excellent. Yes, *bake* is definitely one word we see in our book that has the letter *k* in it. Let's find it. Do we see it here (*pointing to front cover*)? Come up and show me.

CHILD: (*Points to the letter* k *in* Bakes.)

ADULT: Very good. That is the letter *k* in the word *Bakes*. I see another letter *k* in our title. Can you find that one?

CHILD: Here? (*Points to the letter* k *in* Cake.)

ADULT: Wow, very good again. Yes, this is the letter *k* in *Cake* and the letter *k* in *Bakes*. *K* is a very busy letter in our storybook!

Spot Bakes a Cake offers several opportunities to discuss the *function of print*. From the shopping list he and his mother use at the grocery store to the card Spot makes for his father, conversation surrounding the purpose of print is simple to implement. It can be explained that both the list and the card are "handwriting," but that each serves a different purpose. Other instances of environmental print also provide multiple opportunities to discuss the different functions of print.

Sample Dialogue

ADULT: Spot is going to bake his dad a chocolate cake for his birthday. See how he is looking at his grocery list? The list says *flour, butter, eggs,* and *cheese*. What else does the list say if Spot is making a chocolate cake?

CHILDREN: *Cake! Chocolate!*

ADULT: Very good! Yes, here it says *chocolate*. And you know, the list does not say *cake*. I bet Spot and his mom will use the flour to make the cake. Spot and his mom had to make a list of things they need to buy at the store so they don't forget anything. Now look at the print over on this page. Why is there print over here? This print means something different than the list. The list tells Spot what he needs. Anita, can you tell me why there is print over here, too?

CHILD: That's a sign at the store.

ADULT: Right, and the sign says *Special Today Chocolate*. Spot and his mom are lucky. Chocolate is on sale. And here Spot says, "Dad loves chocolate cake!" His arms are full of chocolate. They can cross the word *chocolate* off their list now.

W E E K   1 2

Book: *We're Going on a Bear Hunt*

Targets: Upper- and lower-case forms; page order

Target Definition

- *Upper- and lower-case forms.* Knowledge that letters come in two analogous forms and that there are rules governing when the two forms are used.

- *Page order.* Knowledge of how books are read from front to back and that pages are read from left to right in a two-page spread.

Book Features

We're Going on a Bear Hunt, by Michael Rosen and Helen Oxenbury (1989), is not only a delightful story, but easily adapted into a lesson on *upper- and lower-case forms.* Virtually every page makes distinguishing upper- and lower-case letters an easy topic of conversation with children. Each sentence begins with an upper-case letter in a clear, clean, simple type. In particular, the author's use of "Swishy swashy! Swishy swashy! Swishy swashy!" as the family runs through tall grass offers a terrific opportunity to discuss and compare the upper- and lower-case forms for the letter *s.* After the startling realization that the nose, ears, and eyes in the cave belong to a bear, the text reads "IT'S A BEAR!!!!" This is yet another chance to discuss the letters written in all upper-case form.

Sample Dialogue

ADULT: "Squelch squerch! Squelch squerch! Squelch squerch!" Anita, is this an upper-case *S* or a lower-case *s* (*pointing to the upper-case* S)?

CHILD: Big *S*!

ADULT: You are right. Very good. This is an upper-case *S,* but this is a lower-case *s* (*pointing to the lower-case* s *in* squerch).

This book alternates between having text on both pages of a spread, and then text only on one page, with an illustration on the other page. As a result, the child is given a pattern in determining *page order,* but offered somewhat different formats in which to make this identification.

Sample Dialogue

ADULT: Should I start reading on this page or this page [the left page has text, the right page does not]?

CHILDREN: That page (*indicating page on the left*)!

ADULT: Very good. You noticed that there were words on the left page, and we do need to start there. Let's read our story!

WEEK 13

Book: *Dear Mr. Blueberry*

Targets: Title of book; function of print

Target Definition

- *Title of book.* Knowledge of where the title is located in a book (on the cover and on the title page, typically) and what the function of the title is.

- *Function of print.* Knowledge that the function of print generally is to convey meaning.

Book Features

Dear Mr. Blueberry, by Simon James (1996), is written entirely in the format of letters exchanged between Mr. Blueberry and a child named Emily, who are discussing the possibility of a whale living in the little girl's pond. The *title* is written in script and located toward the bottom of the book's cover. For children accustomed to finding the title at the top of the book, this is a wonderful chance to discuss the fact that the title may actually be located anywhere on the cover of the book.

Sample Dialogue

ADULT: Carolyn, please come up here and show us all where you see the title of the book.

CHILD: I think its here (*points to the title*).

ADULT: You got it. That is the title of our book. What does the title do?

CHILD: Tells us the name of the book.

ADULT: Right again. The title tells us the name of the book and usually gives us clues as to what the book is about.

Since the title of this book is written in script, it provides the occasion to talk about the *function of print* as someone's handwriting, as part of a letter communicating information to someone else. Each page contains a letter either written by Emily or to her from Mr. Blueberry. Conversation can thus continue on letter-writing, salutations (i.e., Dear Mr. Blueberry, Dear Emily), and closing a letter (i.e., Yours Sincerely, Mr. Blueberry; Love, Emily). Each part of the letters offers an example of the function of print.

Sample Dialogue

ADULT: Emily thinks she sees a whale in the pond in her yard, so she writes a letter to Mr. Blueberry to get more information on how to take care of her whale. What do you think she would she like Mr. Blueberry to do when he gets her letter?

CHILD: She wants him to write her a letter about whales.

ADULT: Exactly. Emily thinks Mr. Blueberry knows something about whales and hopes he can teach her something about whales by writing letters back and forth with her. Emily is going to read the words Mr. Blueberry writes in the letter to find out how to take care of her whale.

WEEK 14

Book: *Growing Vegetable Soup*

Targets: Page organization; short words and long words

Target Definition

- *Page organization.* Knowledge of how a page with multiple lines of text is read from top to bottom.

- *Short words and long words.* Knowledge that written words are a distinct unit of print composed of letters (some with many letters and others with few letters).

Book Features

Growing Vegetable Soup, written and illustrated by Lois Ehlert (1987), describes the process of creating and caring for a garden in order to have vegetables to make soup. On almost every page, text begins at the top, thereby easily reinforcing *page organization*. Environmental print labeling—*sun, hand grubber, peas,* and *rake,* for example—occurs throughout the book in conjunction with the story text. Given that these labels are found beside the sun, rake, or worm, or directly on the vegetable, bushel basket, or hand basket, differentiating how one might read environmental print versus story text is made interesting and engaging.

Sample Dialogue

ADULT: Here we read the words *and grow.* These words are at the top of the page and are part of our story. But I see other words on this page. Brian, come up and show me where there are other words on this page.

CHILD: I see a word here and here and here (*pointing to the labels of various vegetables*).

ADULT: Yes, you are right. Very good. I see lots of words down here—some are on a slant, like *potato,* and others are up and down, like *corn* and *carrot.* Brian, show me where we start to read our story on this page.

CHILD: (*Points to a vegetable label.*)

ADULT: Not quite. Here is where we read our story (*points to* and grow *again*). These words tell us what the gardener planted, like we write them on our sticks when we grow our sunflowers. We can look all over the bottom of the page to find these words.

The story *Growing Vegetable Soup* affords the opportunity to compare *short words and long words* such as *pea* with *zucchini, broccoli,* and *pepper.* They all appear on the same page, making direct comparisons convenient and explicit.

Sample Dialogue

ADULT: Look at how long this word is ... *zucchini.* Wow, it has eight letters in it (counting the letters out loud). Let's count the letters in *pea.* There are only three letters in that word *pea.* Which word is longer, *zucchini* or *pea*?

CHILDREN: *Zucchini!* It's longer.

ADULT: You are right. *Zucchini* is a much longer word, actually, than *pea.* It has five more letters than the word *pea* does.

WEEK 15

Book: *Froggy Gets Dressed*

Targets: Letter names; concept of reading

Target Definition

- *Letter names.* Knowledge of the names and corresponding written symbols for the 26 individual letters.

- *Concept of reading.* Knowledge that reading is an act in which persons engage and that reading serves various purposes.

Book Features

Froggy Gets Dressed, by Jonathan London (1992), is the charming story of a boy-frog getting dressed to go outside and play in the snow. Font changes, such as when Froggy's mother calls his name and it appears in upper-case form with large, purple letters, distinguish the letters *F-R-O-G-G-Y* from the uniform black text in which the story is written. In fact, the letters *F-R-O-G-G-Y* are repeated throughout the story, in different fonts, as Froggy's mother calls him in to put on various pieces of clothing he has forgotten. The font changes, along with the repetition of large, easily noticed letters, aids in calling children's attention to *letter names.*

Sample Dialogue

ADULT: Oh, my. Look at Froggy's mother calling for him. She is saying his name *FROGGY!* I see some letters we might know in the word *Froggy.* Martin, what is the name of this letter (*points to* F)?

CHILD: *F!* That is an *F.*

ADULT: *F* is right. *F* is the first letter in Froggy's name. Now what is the name of this letter (*points to* R)?

CHILD: *R!*

ADULT: Right again, that is the letter *R.* Now, do you see any other letters you knew?

CHILD: Yeah, I see an *O.*

ADULT: Yes, right here is an *O.* Very good!

The fact that Froggy keeps forgetting to put on various pieces of clothing contributes to teaching the *concept of reading*. In order to understand why Froggy's mother is calling to him and to know what he has missed, one must continue to read. Having children predict what Froggy might do and then keep reading to find out highlights that the concept of reading includes gaining information about characters and the story plot.

WEEK 16

Book: *I Stink!*

Targets: Concept of letter; page order

Target Definition

- *Concept of letter.* Knowledge about the functions of letters; that letters are units of print that correspond to sounds and are organized to build words.

- *Page order.* Knowledge of how books are read from front to back and that pages are read from left to right in a two-page spread.

Book Features

I Stink!, written by Kate McMullan (2002), is, by its very nature as an alphabet book, useful in calling attention to the *concept of letter*. The "alphabet soup" of which the lead character, a garbage truck, speaks is made up of letters used to spell various items that may be found in garbage cans. These items include "Eggshells," "Fish heads," "Gobs and gobs of gum," and "Half-eaten hot dogs." Children love the unpredictable nature of what the garbage truck might eat, and they enjoy discussing which letter is first in making up these various, funny garbage-worthy items. Each letter of the alphabet is highlighted in a different color than the rest of the word, thus further calling attention to its singular purpose in building a particular word.

Sample Dialogue

ADULT: *Eeeewww,* look at all this garbage that our friend the garbage truck is going to eat. Yuck! Apple cores are first. Look how the word *Apple* starts with the letter *A*. What do we have next? Banana peels. What is the first letter that helps make the word *banana*?

CHILDREN: *B* in *banana!*

ADULT: Yes, that letter *b* is helping make up the word *banana,* and our friend here likes to eat banana peels!

In particular, *I Stink!* has a two-page spread on which one word is written across both pages—"*B-U-R-R-R-P!*" This allows an adult to highlight the importance of *page order,* since reading in anything other than a left-to-right direction will not make sense to the reader.

Sample Dialogue

ADULT: The garbage truck has eaten so much he has to burp. See where it says *BURRRP!* This word is so big that it goes across both pages. We need to start here in order to read the word *BURRRP!* (*points to left page*). Colin, do I start to read the word here or here (*points first to the left page, then to the right page*)?

CHILD: Over there (*indicating left page*).

ADULT: Excellent. Yes, I'm going to read the word *BURRRP* this way (*tracking the word left to right*). He really shouldn't be burping, should he? He should say "Excuse me" after doing that!

WEEK 17

Book: *Animal Action ABC*

Targets: Letters and words; letter names

Target Definition

- *Letters and words.* Knowledge that written words are distinct from the other salient form of print (letters) and that words have meaning.

- *Letter names.* Knowledge of the names and corresponding written symbols for the 26 individual letters.

Book Features

Animal Action ABC, by Karen Pandell (1996), provides the distinction between *letters and words* through font changes for the first letter of each animal action, such as *Arch, Balance,* and *Charge.* With pictures of actual children mimicking the animal action described, along with photos of wildlife engaged in the same practice, words gain meaning easily understandable to young children. *Drink, Eat,* and *Flap* are physical movements easily recreated in the classroom, thus reinforcing the words' meaning.

Sample Dialogue

These children are kicking like the kangaroo does. See them? The word *kick* starts with the letter *k* and ends with the letter *k*. The letter *k* is pretty important in the word *kick*. The word *kick* tells us what the kangaroo can do. Tell me which word the letter *k* makes, Brandon.

CHILD: *Kick!* Like the kangaroo.

ADULT: Yes, the letter *k* makes the word *kick*. And the word *kick* is important because it does what?

CHILD: Tells what the kangaroo does when it fights!

ADULT: Very good. Yes, the letter *k* all by itself doesn't tell us what the kangaroo does, but the word *kick* sure does.

As mentioned before, each alphabet letter is printed in a different font than the rest of the word. As such, the letters stand out from the rest of the text, making the task of finding and discussing *letter names* easier for children.

Sample Dialogue

ADULT: Look at this big green letter. Owen, I bet you recognize this letter. Can you tell us the name of this letter?

CHILD: *O*, like in my name!

ADULT: *O*, just like in your name *Owen*. Very good.

WEEK 18

Book: *My Backpack*

Targets: Upper- and lower-case forms; concept of word in print

Target Definition

- *Upper- and lower-case forms.* Knowledge that letters come in two analogous forms and that there are rules governing when the two forms are used.

- *Concept of word in print.* Knowledge that written words, as a distinct unit of print, map onto spoken words

Book Features

My Backpack, written by Eve Bunting (2005), offers several different opportunities to discuss and point out *upper- and lower-case forms.* The title is printed entirely in upper-case letters, and the first upper-case letter in the first sentence on almost every page is highlighted within a different colored block. The word *PING* is found in environmental print in upper-case form, with the lower-case version on the same page, within the text. Making comparisons between these letter forms can occur naturally during storybook reading.

Sample Dialogue

ADULT: When the little boy presses on the television remote control, it goes *ping.* This is the word *ping,* and it is written in lower-case letters, see … *p-i-n-g, ping.* I see the word *ping* written somewhere else, too, but it looks different. Ian, do you see another word *ping* on this page?

CHILD: (*Points to the illustration.*)

ADULT: That is a picture of the television remote, but I see the word *ping* very close by. Right here. This is the word *PING.* It looks different because it is made up of upper-case letters. The letter *P* looks the same, but see how different the letters *I, N,* and *G* look?

With the main character attempting to fill his backpack with important objects such as socks, a catcher's mitt, a pet kitty, and his mother's shoes, this story is filled with words that reflect a child's daily experience. Calling attention to the *concept of words in print* and highlighting that these written words correspond to familiar spoken words is made relevant and applicable to a child's life.

Sample Dialogue

ADULT: Tell me what this kitty says.

CHILDREN: *Meow!*

ADULT: Kitties do say *meow,* and I see the word *meow* right here. What does this word say?

CHILDREN: *Meow!*

ADULT: Yes, this is the word *meow,* and it is exactly what that kitty will say when the boy puts him in his backpack!

WEEK 19

Book: *Baghead*

Targets: Short words and long words; print direction

Target Definition

- *Short words and long words.* Knowledge that written words are a distinct unit of print composed of letters (some with many letters and others with few letters).

- *Print direction.* Knowledge of how print moves from left to right.

Book Features

Baghead, by Jarrett J. Krosoczka (2002), is the story of a boy who resorts to wearing a paper bag on his head after giving himself a terrible haircut. As he gets ready for school, boards the bus, and arrives at school, several opportunities arise for comparing *short words and long words.* While he is at breakfast, an adult can easily call attention to the number of letters in *of* and *egg* versus *scrambled.* As he gets on the bus, the text reads " 'You can't go to school like that!' she exclaimed." This is a perfect chance to compare three letters in *she* to nine letters in *exclaimed.* Once our character is on the soccer field, his coach asks, " 'How do you plan to play like that?' she demanded." Again, as with the previous example, this is a good occasion to draw a child's attention to the length of the words *she* and *demanded,* especially since they are adjacent to one another.

Sample Dialogue

ADULT: Josh's dad asks him if it was crazy-hat day since Josh has a bag on his head. That is pretty silly, isn't it? *Hat* and *day* have the same number of letters in them. They each have three letters. The word *crazy* has more letters in it. It has five letters in it. Does that mean that *crazy* is a shorter word than *hat* and *day,* or is *crazy* a longer word than *hat* and *day?*

CHILDREN: (*Mix of correct and incorrect responses.*)

ADULT: Since *crazy* has five letters in it, and *hat* and *day* only have three letters in them, the word *crazy* is longer. You can even tell that by looking, since *crazy* and *hat* are side by side on our page.

Although the text in *Baghead* follows the standard horizontal formatting, there are type changes (in style, size, and color) and spacing changes that make discussion and confirmation of *print direction* an engaging task for both adult and child. While not overly complicated, these slight changes aid in bolstering and reinforcing a child's knowledge of this print concept.

Sample Dialogue

ADULT: Olivia, show me which way I read this page.

CHILD: (*Sweeps finger left to right.*)

ADULT: I really like how you knew that, especially since these different size letters might have been confusing. Yes, we read from left to right, just like you showed us.

WEEK 20

Book: *A Color of His Own*

Targets: Page organization; concept of reading

Target Definition

- *Page organization.* Knowledge of how a page with multiple lines of text is read from top to bottom.

- *Concept of reading.* Knowledge that reading is an act in which persons engage and that reading serves various purposes.

Book Features

A Color of His Own, by Leo Lionni (1975), tells the tale of a chameleon dismayed by his change of color each time he changes locations. Text orientation and font do not change, so there is very little distraction when talking about *page organization* with a child. Some pages have only one line of text, whereas others have two or more. This difference across pages opens the door to a conversation about multiple lines of text being read from top to bottom, regardless of the exact number of total lines.

Sample Dialogue

ADULT: It is spring now, and our chameleon walks onto green grass. Before we read the rest of the story, let's look at the print on this page. There are three lines of print on this page (*points to each line while counting*). Sammy, do I start to read on this line or this line (*first points to last line of text, then to the first line of text*)?

CHILD: (*Points to first line of print.*)

ADULT: You are exactly right. I need to start with the top line and keep going until I get to the last line of print.

Given the story line of the chameleon changing color and desiring a color of his own, it is fun to talk with children about what will happen when the chameleon steps on a lemon, a tiger, and best of all, a leaf that changes color in the fall. In order to know what happens to the chameleon, one must continue to engage in the act of reading. It is through the chameleon's journey that the *concept of reading* can be brought up and explored.

Sample Dialogue

ADULT: Our chameleon is having a hard time keeping a color all his own, isn't he? He stepped on a lemon and turned yellow, he stepped on heather and turned purple, then he got stripes after sitting on a tiger! What do you think will happen when he sits on the leaf?

CHILDREN: He's green!

ADULT: Well, to be sure you are right, we are going to have to read the rest of the story to see what happens. Let's read some more.

WEEK 21

Book: *To Market, to Market*

Targets: Word identification; print direction

Target Definition

- *Word identification.* Knowledge of some words in print, including one's own name and other high-frequency or high- function words.

- *Print direction.* Knowledge of how print moves from left to right.

Book Features

With repetition of familiar animal names (e.g., *pig, hen, cow,* and *duck*) and font changes of both color and size, *To Market, to Market,* by Anne Miranda (1997), makes calling attention to *word identification* simple. Children have fun with the rhyme and feel comfortable with the animal names that are highlighted in red type.

Sample Dialogue

ADULT: Here it is again … "Home again, home again, jiggity jig!" Now tell me what this word is (*pointing to* jig)?

CHILDREN: *Jig! Jiggity jig!*

ADULT: *Jig,* yes, this little word is *jig,* and we keep seeing it over and over again. What is this word, all in red?

CHILDREN: *Pig!*

ADULT: Very good. I thought you'd remember that. This word is *pig,* and this word is *jig,* and they rhyme.

With very few orientation changes to the text, *To Market, to Market* is well suited to discuss *print direction.* At one point in the story, our main character loses her patience as the animals she has gotten at the market overrun her kitchen. There are orientation changes to the text when she says "THIS IS THE LAST STRAW!" With each of four lines moving at a diagonal to the next one, it is a good time to point out to children that even though a line of text moves upward at an angle on the page, they still read left to right.

Sample Dialogue

ADULT: Uh-oh, it looks like the lady is getting angry with all the animals in her house. They've made a mess. Look at the words on this page. They are all slanted. This might be a tricky question. Taylor, can you show me which way we read the words on this page?

CHILD: (*Hesitates to answer.*)

ADULT: This is a hard one since some of the words are going up and some are going down. It doesn't matter, though, since we always read left to right, like this (*tracking print with his finger*). Now you try it, Taylor. Follow my finger with yours, and we'll follow the words left to right, just like this.

WEEK 22

Book: *Hey, Little Ant*

Targets: Title of book; upper- and lower-case forms

Target Definition

- *Title of book.* Knowledge of where the title is located in a book (on the cover and on the title page, typically) and what the function of the title is.

- *Upper- and lower-case forms.* Knowledge that letters come in two analogous forms and that there are rules governing when the two forms are used.

Book Features

Hey, Little Ant, written by Phillip and Hannah Hoose (1998), offers an incredibly explicit opportunity to call attention to the *title of the book.* With clear block type, and only three letters set side by side on the cover, it is easy to track the print while reading the title. Other text on the cover is not as obvious, so there is little chance for distraction.

Sample Dialogue

ADULT: OK, LaTisha did a very good job of pointing out the title to us on the cover of our storybook. Who can tell us where else we'll find the title of the book?

CHILDREN: Inside!

ADULT: And what do we call the inside page that has the title of our book on it?

CHILDREN: Title page!

Since this is the story of a conversation between a boy and an ant, each page begins with either *ANT:* or *KID:* to ensure that the reader can easily follow the dialogue. The rest of the text follows the standard sentence format of beginning with an upper-case form, followed by lower-case forms. This makes comparisons between *upper- and lower-case forms* easy to point out.

Sample Dialogue

ADULT: This is interesting. See how this word *ANT* is made up of all upper-case letters? See *A-N-T,* all upper-case letters? Andy, can you come up here and show us where you see another upper-case *A* on this page? This is a hard one!

CHILD: (*Points to letter* A *in* ANT.)

ADULT: Yes, that is an upper-case *A,* for sure. I do see another one, somewhere down here, though. It is hard to find because it is on the picture. Can you see it?

CHILD: Here it is. It's in the book!

ADULT: Wonderful eyes, Andy. Yes, that is another upper-case *A* and that was tricky. Now, let's look for a lower-case *a.* A lower-case *a* looks very different from an upper-case *A.* Can you point to one for us?

CHILD: (*Points to upper-case* O *in text.*)

ADULT: Not quite. That is an upper-case *O.* Here we go. Here is the lower-case *a* in the word *are.* This is the lower-case *a* and this is the upper-case *A* in *ANT.*

WEEK 23

Book: *Mouse Mess*

Targets: Environmental print; page order

Target Definition

- *Environmental print.* Knowledge about the specific and varying functions served by print within the environment (on signs, logos, posters, etc.).

- *Page order.* Knowledge of how books are read from front to back and that pages are read from left to right in a two-page spread.

Book Features

Mouse Mess, written by Linnea Riley (1997), follows the antics of a mouse as he makes himself a snack in a kitchen. *Environmental print* is rife throughout the book, with print on the cereal box, the peanut butter jar, jam jar, and the sardine can.

Sample Dialogue

ADULT: I see some words at the bottom of the page. It looks like there are words on the box in this picture. I think this might be a cereal box. Why do you think there are words on this box, Tammy?

CHILD: So you know what's in the box?

ADULT: Very good! Yes, the box says Corn Flakes on it, so that tells us what kind of cereal is in this box. It is helpful to know that, so we know to pick out the cereal we like.

Page order is one of a few print concepts (along with the concept of words in print, print direction, letter names, and concept of reading) that is fairly easily high-lighted, regardless of a book's print features. *Mouse Mess,* with its catchy rhyming story and block lettering, does offer the clear, simple opportunity for an adult to discuss that books are read from front to back and left to right. For instance, the mouse makes a peanut butter and jelly sandwich, first spreading jam and then smearing the peanut butter. Children have a good time talking about this sequence and have an easy time following it because the story lines that rhyme each fall on a two-page spread.

Sample Dialogue

ADULT: Taylor, help me turn the pages of the book while I read, OK? Come on up here.

CHILD: *(Begins turning pages.)*

ADULT: You are going the right way for us to read our story, but you need to wait for me to read the words on each page before we turn them! Ready? Let's go.

WEEK 24

Book: *In the Small, Small Pond*

Targets: Concept of words in print; print direction

Target Definition

- *Concept of words in print.* Knowledge that written words, as a distinct unit of print, correspond to spoken words.

- *Print direction.* Knowledge of how print moves from left to right.

Book Features

In the Small, Small Pond, by Denise Fleming (1993), describes the movements of various water creatures in the pond they call home. For instance, geese "waddle, wade, ... parade," dragonflies "hover, shiver, wings quiver," and turtles "drowse, doze, eyes close." *Concept of words in print* can be highlighted using these action words to suggest what the animals are doing. Talking about the words, acting them out, and tracking them on the page all enable a child to grasp that written words do correspond to spoken words.

Sample Dialogue

ADULT: Oooo, look at these pretty dragonflies: "hover, shiver, wings quiver." Who has seen a dragonfly? So many of you have! This is the word *quiver.* It is right here. This is what *quiver* means (*motioning with both hands*). It means to shake quickly. Let's all do this and say the word *quiver.*

ADULT AND CHILDREN: (*All motion with hands and say the word* quiver.)

ADULT: Very good. This word tells us the motion that dragonflies make with their wings.

The text in this storybook changes orientation on just about every page. Along with adding excitement and drama to the animals' actions, having children identify *print direction* becomes a bit tricky, but fun, since the text does not follow the standard horizontal format.

Sample Dialogue

ADULT: This page says *lash, lunge, herons plunge.* See how he is putting his head in the water to catch something? Which way do I read this word *lash*? It is slanting upward, isn't it, Rashaun?

CHILD: This way (*tracks word from left to right in upward slant*).

ADULT: Oh, my, that is exactly right. I thought that might be a hard one. Very good. We read words from left to right, just like Rashaun showed us.

WEEK 25

Book: *The Grumpy Morning*

Targets: Letter names; concept of reading

Target Definition

- *Letter names.* Knowledge of the names and corresponding written symbols for the 26 individual letters.

- *Concept of reading.* Knowledge that reading is an act in which persons engage and that reading serves various purposes.

Book Features

The Grumpy Morning, by Pamela Duncan Edwards (1998), tells the story of farm animals looking for their morning meals, as well as some hugs and kisses from the farmer. While the uncomplicated block type makes discussion of *letter names* straightforward and easy to do, on one two-page spread the animals are coming to the farmhouse door, all making their own animal noises. The repetition of letters in *Naa-naa-a, Mooo,* and *Thump-thump* offers a perfect opportunity to compare letter names and reinforce them at the same time.

Sample Dialogue

ADULT: And what does the cow say?

CHILDREN: *Mooo mooo mooo!*

ADULT: She sure does. *Mooo!* And what letter is this (*pointing to the letter* M)?

CHILDREN: *M!*

ADULT: Correct, yes, this is the letter *M* in the word *Mooo.* And what is this letter (*pointing to the letter* o)?

CHILDREN: *O!*

ADULT: Right again. So you'll know this one ...

CHILDREN: *O!*

ADULT: Of course! Yes, this is the letter *o,* and this is the letter *o.* We see it a lot on this page.

Finding out why the farmer has not yet fed her animals and why they have to knock on her door to find her is an engaging way to have children predict what will happen and why. It also is a wonderful way to discuss the *concept of reading* and the fact that they will not find out the answers to these questions unless they keep reading to the end of the story.

Sample Dialogue

Boy, the animals sure do want their breakfast. How are we going to find out if they get their breakfast or not? What must we do?

CHILDREN: Keep reading!

ADULT: Exactly. I have to keep reading the pages in the story to find out what happened to the farmer and whether or not the animals get to eat their breakfast. Let's read!

WEEK 26

Book: *The Noisy Airplane Ride*

Targets: Letters and words; function of print

Target Definition

- *Letters and words.* Knowledge that written words are distinct from the other salient form of print (letters) and that words have meaning.

- *Function of print.* Knowledge that the function of print generally is to convey meaning.

Book Features

The Noisy Airplane Ride, by Mike Downs (2005), makes use of type color and size to highlight words such as *click, ding,* and *thrum-ummmm.* By thus highlighting these individual words, it is easy for an adult to point out the letters in each and discuss the role of *letters* in making up *words.* While each letter standing alone does not convey a particular meaning, together the letters make up words that describe noises commonly heard on an airplane.

Sample Dialogue

ADULT: *Click.* That is the noise the boy heard when he turned on his light to read his book. Click. This word has five letters in it ... *c-l-i-c-k. Click.* Together these letters make the word *Click.* Why does the little boy hear *click* on the plane?

CHILD: Because he clicked the light.

ADULT: Yes, he turned on the light, and it made the sound *click,* and this is the word *click* in the story. This is how we know what sound he heard on the plane. He keeps hearing some very interesting sounds, doesn't he?

With its use of words for the various noises heard while riding in an airplane, this book is well suited to explaining the *function of print*. With words such as stomp, *stomp, tromp, chug, chug,* and *whirrrr,* opportunities abound to discuss the fact that feet make those stomping sounds, the engine of a plane creates the chug, chug we hear, and that the wings make a whirring sound when adjusted. All of these words convey sounds particular to an airplane.

Sample Dialogue

Let's all stomp, stomp, tromp our feet. Stomp, stomp, tromp! Very good. That was easy to hear, wasn't it? Those words aren't quiet words, are they? They are loud words. They tell us the loud noises the little boy is hearing as he gets on the plane. *Stomp, stomp, tromp.* What do these words tell us about getting on the plane?

CHILD: They tell us what the boy hears ... on the plane.

ADULT: They do, don't they? Yes, these words tell us about the sounds we can all listen for when we get on a plane.

WEEK 27

Book: *How to Speak Moo!*

Targets: Title of book; word identification

Target Definition

- *Title of book.* Knowledge of where the title is located in a book (on the cover and on the title page, typically) and what the function of the title is.

- *Word identification.* Knowledge of the some words in print, including one's own name and other high-frequency or high-function words.

Book Features

How to Speak Moo!, by Deborah Fajerman (2002), describes the various ways cows say *moo,* whether sleeping on the ground, riding in a rowboat, or while standing in a tunnel. The *title* is quite prominent on the front cover, with large, clear type.

The title page is particularly interesting to use when discussing the function of a title. Unlike the front cover, the title page has the word *Moo!* in a speech bubble above the heads of four cows. The speech bubble provides a perfect opportunity to address the fact that this book is about what cows say and how they say it.

Sample Dialogue

ADULT: We can also see the title of our book on the title page, remember? Tonya, point to the title of the book on the title page. Here is the title page—can you find the title?

CHILD: (*Points to the title on the title page.*)

ADULT: Very good. That was a little bit harder than other titles we've found here. It looks different, doesn't it? This bubble means all the cows are saying *Moo!*

Repetition of the words *moo* and *cow* make a *word identification* a predictable task for children and thus increases the opportunities for success. Clever changes in spelling, from *moo* to *moooooo* to *mew,* as well as changes in type style, formatting, type size, and orientation, keep everyone on their toes and prevent word identification from becoming too predictable for those children who are ready for a challenge.

Sample Dialogue

ADULT: These cows are jumping up and down on the trampoline. Look at the long word *moooooooooooooooooooooooo* over their heads. Oh, my goodness. Let's count the *o*'s in this word! Twenty-one *o*'s in that word *Moo!* Now look at these words. The word *Mooooo* on the next page only has five *o*'s in it, but it is still the same word *Moo.* Is this shorter form of Moo the same as the longer form of the word?

CHILDREN: Yes! *Moo!*

ADULT: Yes, even with all those *o*'s after the *M,* this is still the same word *Moo* as on this page.

WEEK 28

Book: *Kindergarten Rocks*

Targets: Author of book; environmental print

Target Definition

- *Author of book.* Knowledge of what an author is and where the name of the author is located in a book (on the cover and on the title page, typically); this category also includes children's knowledge of the role of the illustrator.

- *Environmental print.* Knowledge about the specific and varying functions served by print within the environment (on signs, logos, posters, etc.).

Book Features

Kindergarten Rocks, by Katie Davis (2005), offers an opportunity to explain to children the fact that for some books the author not only writes the words for the story, but also draws the pictures, thus serving as *author* and *illustrator.* On both the front cover and the title page, the author's name is represented in clear block type, making location uncomplicated.

Sample Dialogue

ADULT: I see the name *Katie Davis* right here on our storybook for today. Why is her name on the front cover of our storybook?

CHILD: She drew the words!

ADULT: Katie Davis is the author, so she wrote the words. What did Katie Davis do since she is the author?

CHILD: Wrote the words.

ADULT: Yes, she wrote the words. Here it tells us that she also drew the pictures, which means she is also the illustrator.

Since this story is about a young boy's (Dexter) first day of kindergarten, *environmental print* can be found throughout the book. An illustration of a calendar reads *September* with the days of the week, posters in the library say *author, illustrator,* and *I love books!,* and labels denote the location of the *library, playground,* and *cafeteria.* With orientation and type size changes, children will have an engaging time discussing the function of environmental print.

Sample Dialogue

ADULT: Take a look at the pictures that the characters Dexter and his sister Jessica drew. They have words on them. What do you think these words are, Amy? We do this all the time on our pictures that we draw.

CHILD: It's his name. We write our names and stories on our pictures.

ADULT: That is right. This is Dexter's name and this is his sister Jessica's name. They wrote them for the same reason we do, so we know whose picture belongs to whom.

WEEK 29

Book: *The Recess Queen*

Targets: Short words and long words; author of book

Target Definition

- *Short words and long words.* Knowledge that written words are a distinct unit of print composed of letters (some with many letters and others with few letters).

- *Author of book.* Knowledge of what an author is and where the name of the author is located in a book (on the cover and on the title page, typically); this category also includes children's knowledge of the role of the illustrator.

Book Features

The Recess Queen, by Alexis O'Neill (2002), offers numerous opportunities to compare *short words and long words,* with such words as *lollapalooshed* beside *kids* and *as* beside *lightning.* With short and long words adjacent to each other, counting letters and making comparisons becomes an explicit task for children.

Sample Dialogue

ADULT: This is a funny word, *lollapalooshed.* That is a long, long word. It sounds long, doesn't it? Let's count the letters in it (*begins counting while pointing to the individual letters*). The word beside it is shorter, I think. Let's count the letters in the word *kid* (*begins counting letters*). Yes, *lollapalooshed* is a longer word than *kid.* Is *lollapalooshed* a longer word than *kid*?

CHILDREN: Children: Yes!

ADULT: Yes, the word *lollapalooshed,* with 14 letters, is a much longer word than *kid,* with three letters in it.

The names of the story's *author* and *illustrator* are located above the title, thus providing a bit of a challenge to children expecting to find them at the bottom of the front cover, or at least below the title.

Sample Dialogue

ADULT: Laura, come up and show us where the author's name is. This is a little bit different than other places we've found the author's name.

CHILD: (*Points to title of the book.*)

ADULT: That was a hard one. This says *The Recess Queen* and that is the title of our book. The author's name is here, and it says *Alexis O'Neill*. She wrote the words to our story. The name beside hers is *Laura Huliska-Beith,* and she is the illustrator. She drew the pictures. Usually we see the author's name below the title, but this book is different—that is why this question was a hard one.

WEEK 30

Book: *Miss Bindergarten Gets Ready for Kindergarten*

Targets: Concept of word in print; letters and words

Target Definition

- *Concept of word in print.* Knowledge that written words, as a distinct unit of print, correspond to spoken words.

- *Letters and words.* Knowledge that written words are distinct from the other salient form of print (letters) and that words have meaning.

Book Features

Miss Bindergarten Gets Ready for Kindergarten, written by Joseph Slate (1996), utilizes type color and style changes to highlight the first letter of each kindergarten student's name. Each name, therefore, stands out from the other words and provides a pattern by which children can identify these names and discuss the *concept of words in print.*

Sample Dialogue

ADULT: These words say *Matty Lindo.* That is our character's name. He is looking out of the window of the school bus. I bet his friends call him *Matty* when he goes to school. What is this character's name?

CHILDREN: *Matty! Matty Lindo!*

ADULT: Yes, that is right. This boy's name is Matty Lindo, and he is on the school bus. These words tell us his name.

Just as the type color and style changes highlight the characters' entire names within the body of the text, these differences also call attention to the first letter of each name, providing a good opportunity to discuss the concept of *letters and words*. It is made clear within the text that the letter *B* in *Brenda* is not only distinct from the name, but from every other word that follows the short sentence.

Sample Dialogue

ADULT: This is the letter *B*. This is a big, upper-case letter *B*. It makes the word *Brenda*, and that is this little girl's name. She is brushing her teeth. This big letter *B* helps make the name *Brenda*. What does the letter *B* do here?

CHILD: Makes her name.

ADULT: Yes, this letter *B* helps make the word *Brenda*, and that is this little girl's name. Her parents and her friends all call her *Brenda* because that is her name.

CHAPTER 5

Scaffolding Children's Learning
Using High and Low Support Strategies

In this chapter we discuss how adults can support, or *scaffold*, children's development of print knowledge. As adults begin to incorporate a more systematic focus on print within their reading interactions with children—as occurs when they call attention to print—it is both necessary and important to give children the support they need to learn and profit from these experiences. This support is so important to a high-quality implementation of the calling attention to print technique that we have coupled specific scaffolding techniques (high- and low-support strategies) with each print-knowledge target on the STAR cards presented in Appendix C. In this chapter we provide an overview of how adult readers can effectively scaffold children's interactions with print using high- and low-support strategies.

SCAFFOLDING

The term *scaffolding* has been a part of our teaching lexicon since the mid-1970s (e.g., Wood & Middleton, 1975), and it is based on the seminal writings of Vygotsky (1930/1978), a Russian psychologist who was a contemporary of Piaget. Generally speaking, scaffolding is an *instructional action* taken by a more knowledgeable partner, such as a parent, teacher, or peer, that is carefully designed to facilitate a child's learning. The instructional action takes into account the ways in which children build a base of knowledge incrementally by carefully considering how much support a child needs in a particular activity or task to be successful (O'Connor, Notari-Syverson, & Vadasy, 1998). Some children, to be successful in a task, require high levels of support, whereas other children may require only minimal levels. The skilled instructor can discern how much support a child needs in a particular type of task and offer exactly that amount of support.

With respect to the focus of this book, which concerns how to promote children's development of print knowledge, each child encounters the world of print and storybook reading with differing levels of background knowledge and experience (Justice & Ezell, 2004). For some children, concepts such as author, title, and print direction, as well as the fact that print conveys meaning, are as ingrained in their minds as the name of their favorite pet or stuffed animal. For others, these concepts are mysteries yet to be understood. When asked to show which way one should read the words on the page, a child with no knowledge of print direction may run his or her finger from right to left, or even from the top of the page to the bottom of the page. This child would benefit from the instructional action of an adult who offers a high level of support—an action that would help the child successfully show which way print is read on a page. In this particular instance, an instructional action offering a high level of support would be situated within the child's zone of proximal development.

ZONE OF PROXIMAL DEVELOPMENT

An instructional action or teaching episode occurs when an adult engages a child in a task that is currently beyond his or her capabilities. By employing the technique of scaffolding within this episode, the adult is able to directly and explicitly facilitate the child's acquisition of the skill, such as demonstrating print direction, which would be too difficult for the child to complete on his or her own. Russian psychologist Lev Vygotsky described this process as working within the child's *zone of proximal development* (1930/1978). When working within the child's zone, the adult takes into account the current dynamic state of a child's developmental capacity and then facilitates that process by offering the necessary supports so that the child can achieve success. Vygotsky believed that "the only 'good learning' is that which is in advance of development" (1930/1978, p. 89), such that *learning must precede development*. Other more static models of learning only account for what a child has already mastered and do not view learning as preceding a child's development. Vygotsky took matters one step further by emphasizing the point that teaching must occur prior to actual skill acquisition. He described a child's nascent abilities as "the 'buds' or 'flowers' of development rather than the 'fruits' of development" (Vygotsky, 1930/1978, p. 86). Following this metaphor, the adult is tasked with nurturing and watering those buds and flowers until they mature. Scaffolding can be considered the nurturing and the watering along the way to maturation, or skill acquisition.

An important premise of Vygotskian theory is that as the child progresses along the path to mastery, the adult gradually removes him- or herself from a supporting role; this is referred to as *sensitive withdrawal*. Adult use of sensitive withdrawal during various childhood tasks has been observed to stimulate children's takeover of a task and to improve their subsequent independent performance (Diaz, Neal, & Vachio, 1991).

PSYCHOLOGICAL PROCESSES WITHIN THE ZONE OF PROXIMAL DEVELOPMENT

When a child attempts to learn something new and the learning is situated within his or her zone of proximal development, the task (i.e., what is being learned) is too difficult for the child to complete on his or her own. However, by working with a more knowledgeable adult or peer who scaffolds his or her performance, the child is able to exhibit learning in the context of assistance. According to Vygotskian theory and social-interactionist accounts of learning, children's learning occurs first on an external and socially mediated plane (see Figure 5.1) and, over time, moves inward to an internal and psychological plane. This process can be likened to the adult leading the child through a complicated dance, with toes sometimes getting stepped on along the way. Think of the adult as holding the child's hands while teaching the dance steps. Gradually, as the child learns the movements and takes ownership of them, the adult should begin to release his or her grasp. This does not mean that balance is not provided at key moments when needed, but eventually, the child is able to dance on his or her own, enjoying the freedom of movement in a task now well mastered. The dance

Stage 1. The interpersonal (social or external) plane
Characteristics of children's conceptual performance: • Dependent on social context within a collaborative activity • Mediated by their own developmental level • Scaffolded by a more capable and knowledgeable peer
Stage 2. The intrapersonal (psychological or internal) plane
Characteristics of children's conceptual performance: • Independent of a social context • Mediated by their own developmental level • Automatized and regulated by self

FIGURE 5.1. Development as a two-stage process: A Vygotskian perspective.

steps have been internalized; the freedom of movement comes from the child's "ownership" of a skill that was once too difficult to complete on his or her own.

Applying these points to our context of print knowledge, children's development of emerges initially through their interactions with others in a social context (Blanc, 1990; Justice & Ezell, 1999; Vygotsky, 1934/1986). Their abstract understanding of what print is (its functions) and what it looks like (its forms) are learned through the support of others, and this knowledge initially resides wholly within an external and social plane of development. However, over time, these external functions move inward as children's knowledge becomes internalized and more fully developed. Along the way to mastery (i.e., internalization of knowledge from the external to the internal plane), the adult fosters children's development by linking the level of scaffolding to the level of their knowledge. When children's knowledge exists primarily on an external plane, in that they can demonstrate knowledge only with the assistance of another, the adult uses high-support strategies. As the child gains ground on internalizing the skill, so that knowledge exists primarily on an internal plane, the adult reduces the level of support, utilizing low-support strategies to allow the child more independence in achieving success.

In the next sections we provide descriptions of specific types of high- and low-support strategies that adults can use when developing children's print knowledge by calling attention to print. We have adopted these terms and their definitions from the work of O'Connor and colleagues (1998).

HIGH-SUPPORT STRATEGIES

High-support strategies are required for tasks that are very difficult for children and that they are far from being able to do on their own, because their knowledge is relatively unrefined and exists solely on an external plane (Notari-Syverson et al., 1998). Effective scaffolding within the zone of proximal development, when engaging children in tasks that are very difficult and unfamiliar to them, incorporates interactions marked by "demonstration, leading questions, and by introducing the initial elements of the task's solution" (Moll, 1990, p. 11). It is for this reason that our high-support strategies follow a general rule of thumb: *High support always involves the adult providing the correct answer to a question before turning to children for response.* Once the children have responded, the adult then reiterates the answer for further clarification. Let's turn now to a description of four high-support strategies utilized when calling attention to print: modeling the answer, eliciting the answer, coparticipation, and reducing choices/giving alternatives (see Figure 5.2).

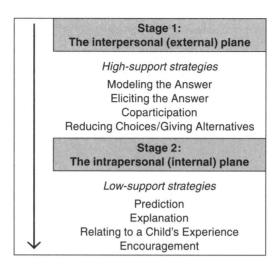

FIGURE 5.2. Strategies associated with plane of knowledge (external vs. internal).

Modeling the Answer

When employing this technique, the adult engages in self-talk in order to make the process of answering as explicit as possible. *Self-talk* refers to the practice of the adult talking through the problem aloud, in order to model the process of finding solutions for the children. The end product of self-talk is always the correct answer to the question. Once the adult has finished modeling the answer, the very same question should be posed to the child. For example:

ADULT: I'm going to look for some letters on this page. I need to find where the print or words are on this page. Here are some words at the very top of the page. And I know that each word is made up of letters. Here are some letters, right here in this word (*pointing to each letter individually*). Addie, please come up here and show me where I can find some letters on this page.

CHILD: (*Points to the letters.*)

ADULT: Very good. You knew you had to find where the print or where the words were on the page in order to find some letters.

In this example, the adult used self-talk to guide children's attention to the process of picking out individual letters. After the child successfully found the letters, the adult reinforced this answer by repeating the process. Here is another example:

ADULT: I wonder what this book is about. If I want to find out, I need to look on the cover and find the title. Here's the title. I recognize a few words in this title. This word is *duck*. I bet this book is going to be about ducks! Cole, what is one way I can find out what my book is going to be about?

CHILD: Look at the pictures!

ADULT: I can look at the pictures, but when I was wondering what this book was about, I also looked for the title. How did I know what the book was about?

CHILD: You looked at the title.

ADULT: Yes! You are right. I looked at the title of the book since I know that that title tells me what the book is about.

Although the child in this example did not initially provide the correct response to the question, the adult reiterated the process of finding out what the book was about, thus providing the answer as to the role of the title. Notice how she asked the question again and then gave positive feedback, along with a third explanation of how to find out what a book is about.

Eliciting the Answer

This strategy is one of the simplest ways to provide high support for a child. The adult draws direct attention to the desired print target, and, after explicitly labeling the feature(s), asks the child to provide the very same response or label. For example:

ADULT: Take a look at the title of this book. It says "I Stink!" And in the title I see the letter *I* here and here (*pointing to both* I*'s in the title*). OK now, what letter am I pointing to right now?

CHILDREN: *I!*

ADULT: You are exactly right. I am pointing to the *I* in the title "I Stink!"

In this example, the adult has actually provided two explicit supports for the children. First, she provides the answer to the question she will ask the children. Second, she provides the support of pointing to the letter, herself, when asking the children what letter it is. By doing so, she keeps their focus on letter identification, rather than asking them the additional task of remembering exactly which letter she had found. Note how the adult again labels the letter *I* after the children answer her question. Here is another example of this technique:

ADULT: This word is *jungle*. Look right here at this word I'm pointing to. This word is *jungle*. You tell me what this word is.

CHILDREN: *Jungle!*

ADULT: You got it! The word I'm pointing to is jungle.

As in the first example, the adult continues to point to the word *jungle* in order to reinforce just which word she is asking them to identify. And, again, she repeats the answer to her request.

Coparticipation

Coparticipation offers a way to actively involve children in the process of engaging with print. It can be implemented in a variety of ways, such as asking a child to point to something in the book, manipulate the book, or call out answers to a question. For example:

ADULT: This is the letter *J (pointing to the letter)*. Beth, can you point to the letter *J* for me?

CHILD: It looks like this one, with a curl on it (*pointing to the* J)!

ADULT: Yes, that is the letter *J*! It does look like a curl, doesn't it? That is a *J*. Let's make a *J* together with our fingers. Watch me!

In this example, note how there are two types of coparticipation occurring in order to focus on letter identification. After the child is asked to point to the letter in the book, the adult takes advantage of the child's comment that the letter *J* has a "curl" on it. Both adult and child make the shape of a *J* in the air, thus reinforcing the shape of that letter. Here is another example:

ADULT: These three words look shorter than the word *sprouts*, don't they? Let's count the letters in the shorter words together. (*Begins counting the letters in* in, and, all, *and the* with the children.) Now let's count the letters in *sprouts* together. (*Begins counting with the children.*) Seven letters in *sprouts* and only three letters in our other words. Who can tell me which is longer, *sprouts* (*pointing to the word*) or *the* (*pointing to the word*)?

CHILDREN: *Sprouts!*

ADULT: Exactly. We counted the letters in *sprouts*, and it had seven. The other words only had three letters in them. *Sprouts* is definitely the longest word. Seven is more than three!

Although definitely a noisier way to call attention to print, counting together is a fun, concrete way to distinguish long words from short words. Note how the adult repeats the reason that *sprouts* is the longest word—after counting up the letters "seven is more than three!"

Reducing Choices/Giving Alternatives

By giving the child a choice between two response options, the adult provides high support by focusing the child's attention on specific features of print. The correct answer should always be included as one of the choices provided. This can sometimes be, however, a more rigorous high-support task in that the child must compare and contrast the alternatives before providing an answer. The adult has provided the answer, as required under our definition of high-support, but it is comingled with a "decoy" or incorrect answer. For example:

ADULT: Which letter is the *M*? Is it this one (*pointing to* M) or is it this one (*pointing to* L)?

CHILD: M (*calling out as the adult points to the* L)!

ADULT: This is not the letter *L*. I'm pointing to the letter *M* right now. This is the *M*.

Notice that the adult in this example does not engage in eliciting the answer by providing the answer first on its own. Reducing choices/giving alternatives is just that—the correct answer is provided, but matched against an incorrect response. It is important that the correct answer is always provided for the child, whether it is in the form of an adult correction or a repetition of the child's correct answer. Here is another example of reducing choices/giving alternatives:

ADULT: I'm looking for a word on this page. Is this a word (*pointing to a word*) or is this a word (*pointing to one of the items in the backpack*)?

CHILD: That's not a word. He put that in his backpack!

ADULT: He did put that in his backpack, you are right. It's a picture, not a word. This is the word.

This example highlights the usefulness of this strategy in providing concrete evidence of the nonexample. Unlike the first example, which was a little more difficult given that both choices were letters, the second example is between that of a clear example—the printed word—and a nonexample—the illustration.

The high-support strategies offered here can be used in many different ways to scaffold print referencing skills that are new and unfamiliar for children. Here are some general tenets to keep in mind when using these techniques:

1. Always remember *to provide the answer before* asking the child.

2. After the child has answered, be sure to either *repeat the correct answer he or she has supplied or offer the correct response* if an incorrect one was given.

3. High-support techniques are always explicit and require the *least amount of work for the child*.

4. It is useful to *match explicit language and questioning with physical supports*, such as tracking and pointing, in order to reinforce concepts.

LOW-SUPPORT STRATEGIES

When employing low-support strategies, the adult serves less as a model, as someone to be imitated, and more as a guide who is challenging a child to apply knowledge that is already owned on an internal plane. Low-support strategies are appropriate for use when engaging a child in a teaching episode that seeks to foster higher-order responses. In contrast to the high-support strategies described before, low-support techniques make use of primarily open-ended questions. The four strategies described here acknowledge that the child, although not yet a master of a specific knowledge domain, has been exposed to the targeted concepts and may be on the way to mastery of the desired skill. Adult support must be adjusted to accommodate the child's growing independence. However, just as with high-support techniques, the adult repeats and may even extend the child's response to continue the feedback loop that is at the heart of the interactive nature of storybook reading and scaffolding. After all, the practice of scaffolding rests "on the social system within which we hope children learn, with the understanding that this social system is mutually and actively created by teacher and students" (Moll, 1990, p. 11). The four low-support strategies utilized when calling attention to print include prediction, explanation, relating to a child's experience, and encouragement (see Figure 5.2).

Prediction

The strategy of predicting can almost be seen as that of guessing, which children love, especially when put in the form of a game. This is a higher-order activity in that an answer has not been immediately offered before the question, and it requires children to recall a concept or skill to which they've previously been exposed. Here is an example:

ADULT: How am I going to tell what my book is going to be about? Anita, can you tell me?

CHILD: You can see if you know any words in the title.

ADULT: Excellent. If I want to know about the book, all I have to do is look at the title. The title of this book is *We're Going on a Bear Hunt*. Hmmm, what do you think this is about?

CHILDREN: Bears!

ADULT: I think so too. Let's read on and find out.

Though this young child is not reading the actual text at this point, the role of the title is clearly understood. The adult reinforces this knowledge by reading the title and asking the children for another prediction about content. Here is another example:

ADULT: We've learned lots of things about how to read a book, haven't we? There are lots of things to do when we read, aren't there? What would I have to do first, before I can read a book?

CHILD: Pick a book!

ADULT: Exactly. I need to choose a book. Then what do I have to do to read a book?

CHILD: Choose a book.

ADULT: Yep, that's what I'm going to do first. And then what do we do?

CHILD: We look at the title!

ADULT: That's right, we look at the title, right here. Now, if I wanted to sneak a peek at the last page of my book, what should I do?

CHILD: Do it this way to peek. (*Turns pages to the end of the book.*)

ADULT: Now I can peek at the last page! And to get there, I turn the pages just the way you showed me.

The adult in this example has accomplished two print-referencing tasks: She has addressed the process of reading in the questions concerning choosing a book and looking at the title first, and she has highlighted print direction. Notice that she does not provide the answers to her questions, but rather gives small prompts to guide children to their answers. The first prompt comes by mentioning that they've learned a lot about "how to read a book," and the second comes when she wants to know how to "sneak a peek at the last page." Though the children are comfortable with these tasks and have produced the desired answers, the adult still confirms and repeats the correct responses.

Explanation

Using this technique allows the adult to expand and extend a child's response by adding more information to further solidify the concept or skill. Along with reinforcing the answer to a specific question, the adult draws the child's attention back to the text for confirmation. The print features of the text can be used to show the child that there is support for his or her answers. Here is an example:

ADULT: What is this word?

CHILD: *Stop!*

ADULT: You're right. It says *stop* (*pointing to the word*). We know that because we know that this is a stop sign that tells cars to stop. Cars need to stop when they see this sign so that there is not an accident.

The adult is using two means of explanation in this particular example. The child can recognize the stop sign, having seen it numerous times, so word identification has been addressed. The fact that print carries meaning is conveyed in the adult's last utterance, which adds significant purpose to what the sign actually says. Here is another example:

ADULT: Does anyone know what words are made of?

CHILDREN: Letters!

ADULT: That's right! Words are made up of lots of different letters. And you will see the same letter can be used to make up different words, like *c* is in *cat* and *c* is in *cart*.

In this example the children understand the general role of letters in making up words. To carry the point one step further, the adult offers an example of the specific role of the letter *c* in making up two different words. This accentuates the target of concept of letter.

Relating to a Child's Experience

Utilizing a child's own experiences and background knowledge is a powerful way to reinforce learning, especially when the child is headed toward mastery of a concept. Relating print concepts to extratextual features and ideas places this technique within the boundaries of low support. The child is required to supply the answer to an open-ended question without necessarily having direct support from either the storybook or the adult. Here is an example:

ADULT: The word *baby* has two *b*'s in it. Can you think of another word that has the letter *b* in it? Bobby, I bet you'll be able to!

CHILD: My name, *Bobby!*

ADULT: That's right! Your name has three *b*'s in it. That letter is very busy helping to make your name.

Children enjoy using the letters in their name to generalize to other words. Since these are the letters a child is likely to know first, using this technique to highlight these connections is fun and easy to use. Another example is:

ADULT: What is this word right here, over the animal's head? Remember when Mr. Mitchell brought his sheep to school so we could see him and ask questions about him? What did that sheep say?

CHILDREN: *Baaa baaa!*

ADULT: You remember! That's right. So, if there are words over this sheep's head in our book, what do you think they say?

CHILDREN: *Baaa baaa!*

The adult in this example has taken advantage of an extracurricular activity to highlight a word in the storybook. By referencing this activity, the children's background knowledge is activated, and they can apply that information to the storybook text.

Encouragement

When using this strategy, the adult's ultimate goal is to encourage the child to produce an answer to a question that he or she has already answered before with success. The language used reminds children that they are familiar with this task and have the correct response at their fingertips, so to speak. Here is an example:

ADULT: Timothy, I saw you reading one of the books in our classroom the other day. You were reading to a friend and turning the pages. Come on up here and show me which way I should turn the pages.

CHILD: (*Models how to correctly turn the pages.*)

ADULT: Thank you so much for showing us how we need to turn the pages in order to read our book.

With encouragement and praise, the adult in this interaction has shown the child that the information provided is correct and that it is useful for reading. Here is another example:

ADULT: You all did such a good job yesterday picking out upper-case letters and lower-case letters. Remember how much fun we had calling out upper-case or lower-case? We're going to do that again today. When I point to a letter, I want you to call out whether that letter is upper-case or lower-case, OK? Let's start.

By providing a familiar task and reminding children of the good job they did before, as well as the fun they had, the adult has set the stage for a safe, comfortable environment in which the children can test their newfound skill.

As with our high-support strategies, the low-support strategies offered here can be used in many different ways to scaffold children's learning of print-knowledge objectives with which they are familiar and over which they are gaining mastery. Here are some general tenets to keep in mind when using these techniques:

1. Low-support strategies *do not initially provide the answer* to the child.

2. As with high-support strategies, always be sure to either *repeat the correct answer the child has supplied or offer the correct response* if an incorrect one was given.

3. Low-support techniques are less explicit than high-support techniques and require the *most amount of work for the child.*

4. *It is not necessary to provide the child with physical supports* such as tracking and pointing to support an answer.

REFLECTIVE IMPLEMENTATION

As one uses print-referencing strategies and seeks to differentiate instruction when reading storybooks with heterogeneous groups of children, it is important to reflect upon the extent to which differing supports were offered to children. This reflection is necessary because storybook-reading interactions are complex events that unfold in dynamic ways. It can be difficult to offer each child within a reading session the opportunity to participate at the level most appropriate to his or her skills and interests. For this reason, it may be useful for educators, upon completing a book-reading session, to jot down notes (informally or formally) regarding use of various types of supports with different participating children. A sample of such a note-taking system is presented in Figure 5.3. The benefits of such a system are twofold. First, this system can help calibrate use of different types of supports. In our work with teachers, we have found that sometimes teachers perceive that they use one type of strategy (e.g., reducing alternatives) much more often than they actually do. In this way, a note-taking system can help teachers calibrate what they perceive themselves to be doing with what they are actually doing.

	Low-Support Strategies				High-Support Strategies			
	Prediction	Explanation	Relating	Encouragement	Modeling	Eliciting	Coparticipating	Reducing choices
Amber	✓	✓						
Inez		✓	✓			✓		
Jill						✓	✓	✓
Juarez C						✓		✓
Juarez M			✓	✓				
Laura		✓	✓	✓				
Melissa							✓	
Rashaun					✓			
Seam		✓	✓					
Shayne						✓	✓	
Vera						✓	✓	
Veronica			✓	✓		✓		

FIGURE 5.3. Note-taking system for tracking use of high- and low-support strategies.

Second, adopting some sort of note-taking or data-collection system that tracks one's use of different support strategies can be helpful for thinking about individual children's responsiveness to specific types of strategies over time. This method is particularly useful for assuring that one reduces support from high levels to low levels as a child gains mastery of specific concepts or skills. Undoubtedly, children will show substantial individual differences in the pace with which they develop their knowledge of different dimensions of print knowledge, and teachers will want to be responsive to these individual differences. In so doing, teachers will play an important role in helping children develop a strong foundation of knowledge about print that will ease their transition to beginning reading within the context of formal schooling.

Trade Books for Calling Attention to Print

Title	PSM	Genre	Interesting Features	Citation
Rumble in the Jungle	1.75	Narrative	Change in font, type orientation; environmental print	Andreae, D., & Wojtowycz, D. (1996). *Rumble in the jungle*. London: Little Tiger Press.
The Dandelion Seed	1.31	Narrative	Change in type size, bold font	Anthony, J. (1997). *The dandelion seed*. Nevada City, CA: Dawn.
The Mitten	0	Narrative	Type consistent; illustrations foreshadow story events	Brett, J. (1989). *The mitten*. New York: Scholastic.
Clifford Goes to Dog School	0.76	Narrative	Environmental print	Bridwell, N. (2002). *Clifford goes to dog school*. New York: Scholastic.
My Backpack	1.38	Narrative	Change in type color, size; environmental print	Bunting, E. (2005). *My backpack*. Honesdale, PA: Boyds Mills Press.
The Way I Feel	2.18	Informational	Change in font, type color, size, and orientation	Cain, J. (2000). *The way I feel*. Seattle: Parenting Press.
Never Spit on Your Shoes	2.23	Narrative	Environmental print	Cazet, D. (1990). *Never spit on your shoes*. New York: Orchard Books.
A Lime, a Mime, and a Pool of Slime	5.18	Informational	Change in type color	Cleary, B. P. (2006). *A lime, a mime, and a pool of slime*. Minneapolis: Millbrook Press.

Note. PSM = print salience metric. To calculate PSM, or the average number of print-salient elements per page, (1) determine the total number of story pages, (2) count the number of instances that print is embedded in the illustrations, (3) count the number of type changes in the body of text, and (4) add the values from steps 2 and 3 and divide by the value from step 1.

Title	PSM	Genre	Interesting Features	Citation
Giggle, Giggle, Quack	0.62	Narrative	Environmental print	Cronin, D. (2002). *Giggle, giggle, quack*. New York: Scholastic.
I'm Gonna Like Me	3.8	Other	Change in font, type orientation; environmental print	Curtis, J. L. & Cornell, L. (2002). *I'm gonna like me*. New York: Joanna Cotler Books.
Big Words for Little People	4.33	Informational	Change in type color, capitalization, font; environmental print	Curtis, J. L., & Cornell, L. (2008). *Big words for little people.* New York: Joanna Cotler Books.
Where Do Balloons Go?	2.5	Narrative	Environmental print	Curtis, J. L. (2000). *Where do balloons go?* New York: Joanna Cotler Books.
Monster Mess	1.66	Narrative	Change in type size, orientation	Cuyler, M. (2008). *Monster mess*. New York: Margaret K. McElderry Books.
One Ridonculous Adventure	1.63	Narrative	Change in font, type color, orientation	Daly, C. (2008). *One ridonculous adventure*. New York: Disney Press.
Kindergarten Rocks!	4.16	Narrative	Change in font, type size color; environmental print	Davis, K. (2005). *Kindergarten rocks!* New York: Harcourt.
Llama Llama Red Pajama	1.28	Narrative	Change in font and type color	Dewdney, A. (2005). *Llama llama red pajama*. New York: Penguin.
Llama Llama Mad at Mama	1.94	Narrative	Change in font and type color	Dewdney, A. (2007). *Llama llama mad at mama*. New York: Penguin.
The Noisy Airplane Ride	1.93	Mixed	Environmental print	Downs, M. (2005). *The noisy airplane ride*. Berkeley, CA: Tricycle Press.
The Grumpy Morning	0.67	Narrative	Environmental print	Edwards, P. D. (1998). *The grumpy morning*. New York: Scholastic.
Growing Vegetable Soup	3.3	Mixed	Environmental print	Ehlert, L. (1987). *Growing vegetable soup*. San Diego: Harcourt.
Red Leaf, Yellow Leaf	1.11	Mixed	Environmental print	Ehlert, L. (1991). *Red leaf, yellow leaf*. New York: Scholastic.
The Letters Are Lost	3.86	Narrative	Change in font, type color and size; environmental print	Ernst, L. C. (1996). *The letters are lost*. New York: Scholastic.

Title	PSM	Genre	Interesting Features	Citation
How to Speak Moo!	2.21	Narrative	Environmental print	Fajerman, D. (2002). *How to speak moo!* Hauppauge, NY: Barron's.
Clifford for President	1.1	Narrative	Environmental print	Figueroa, A. (2004). *Clifford for president*. New York: Scholastic.
In the Small, Small Pond	0.79	Narrative	Change in type orientation and size	Fleming, D. (1993). *In the small, small pond*. New York: Henry & Holt.
Jamboree Day	0.34	Narrative	Italic font	Greene, R. G. (2001). *Jamboree day*. New York: Scholastic.
My First Day of School	4.34	Narrative	Environmental print	Hallinan, P. K. (1987). *My first day of school*. Nashville, TN: Ideals Children's Books.
Spot Bakes a Cake	0.73	Narrative	Environmental print	Hill, E. (1994). *Spot bakes a cake*. New York: Puffin.
Hey, Little Ant!	1.32	Other	Bold font; environmental print	Hoose, P. M., & Hoose, H. (1998). *Hey, little ant!* Berkeley, CA: Tricycle Press.
When Daddy's Truck Picks Me Up	1	Narrative	Environmental print	Hunter, J. N. (2006). *When daddy's truck picks me up*. Morton Grove, IL: Albert Whitman.
Dear Mr. Blueberry	1	Narrative	Change in font	James, S. (1996). *Dear Mr. Blueberry*. New York: Aladdin.
The Little Bit Scary People	1.93	Mixed	Change in font	Jenkins, E. (2008). *The little bit scary people*. New York: Hyperion Books for Children.
The Emperor's Egg	1.33	Informational	Change in type orientation, italic font	Jenkins, M. (1999). *The emperor's egg*. Cambridge: Candlewick Press.
Move	3.21	Informational	Change in type orientation and size	Jenkins, S. & Page, R. (2006). *Move*. Boston: Houghton Mifflin.
Actual Size	1.21	Informational	Bold font and change in type size	Jenkins, S. (2004). *Actual size*. Boston: Houghton Mifflin.
Animal Band	1.57	Narrative	Change in font, type orientation, and color	Jennings, C. S. (2007). *Animal band*. New York: Sterling.
In the Night Garden	1.66	Narrative	Environmental print, italic font	Joosse, B. (2008). *In the night garden*. New York: Henry Holt.
Do Unto Otters	3.97	Mixed	Environmental print, change in font	Keller, L. (2007). *Do unto otters*. New York: Henry Holt.

Title	PSM	Genre	Interesting Features	Citation
The Scrambled States of America Talent Show	9.28	Mixed	Environmental print; change in type color, orientation	Keller, L. (2008). *The scrambled states of America talent show.* New York: Henry Holt.
Guess What I Found in Dragon Wood?	1.6	Narrative	Environmental print; change in type size	Knapman, T. (2007). *Guess what I found in dragon wood?* New York: Bloomsbury U.S.A. Children's Books.
The Biggest Snowman Ever	0.16	Narrative	Environmental print	Kroll, S. (2005). *The biggest snowman ever.* New York: Scholastic.
Baghead	1.07	Narrative	Change in font and type size	Krosoczka, J. J. (2002). *Baghead.* New York: Random House.
M Is for Music	5.65	Informational	Environmental print; change in font	Krull, K. (2003). M *is for music.* New York: Harcourt.
Little Smudge	0.9	Narrative	Change in type size and orientation	Le Neouanic, L. (2005). *Little smudge.* New York: Sterling.
A Color of His Own	0	Narrative	Type consistent and sparse	Lionni, L. (1975). *A color of his own.* New York: Scholastic.
Doctor Meow's Big Emergency	1.79	Narrative	Environmental print	Lloyd, S. (2007). *Doctor meow's big emergency.* New York: Henry Holt.
How to Be a Baby	1.94	Narrative	Environmental print; change in capitalization	Lloyd-Jones, S., & Heap, S. (2007). *How to be a baby.* New York: Schwartz & Wade Books.
Froggy Gets Dressed	1.79	Narrative	Change in font, type size, and color	London, J. (1992). *Froggy gets dressed.* New York: Puffin.
Once I Ate a Pie	3.17	Narrative	Change in type size, bold font	MacLachlan, P., & Charest, E. M. (2006). *Once I ate a pie.* New York: Joanna Cotter Books.
Chicka Chicka Boom Boom	6.5	Narrative	Environmental print, bold font	Martin, B. Jr., & Archambault, J. (1989). *Chicka chicka boom boom.* New York: Scholastic.
Marveltown	1.04	Narrative	Environmental print, change in font	McCall, B. (2008). *Marveltown.* New York: Farrar, Straus & Giroux.
Superhero ABC	9.28	Narrative	Change in font, environmental print	McLeod, B. (2006). *Superhero ABC.* New York: HarperCollins.
I Stink!	5.1	Mixed	Change in type size, orientation, and color	McMullan, K. (2002). *I stink!* New York: HarperCollins.

Title	PSM	Genre	Interesting Features	Citation
To Market, to Market	3.66	Narrative	Change in type size, color, and capitalization; environmental print	Miranda, A. (1997). *To market, to market*. San Diego: Voyager Books.
Down by the Cool of the Pool	4.13	Narrative	Change in font	Mitton, T. (2001). *Down by the cool of the pool*. New York: Orchard Books.
Monkey with a Tool Belt	4.23	Narrative	Environmental print	Monroe, C. (2008). *Monkey with a tool belt*. New York: Carolrhoda Books.
I Like It When …	0.35	Narrative	Environmental print	Murphy, M. 1997). *I like it when …* San Diego: Harcourt.
The Very Sleepy Sloth	1.21	Narrative	Change in font, type orientation, and capitalization	Murray, A. (2003). *The very sleepy sloth*. New York: Scholastic.
Tex and Sugar: A Big City Kitty Ditty	1.69	Narrative	Environmental print	Newman, B. J. (2007). *Tex and Sugar: A big city kitty ditty*. New York: Sterling.
The Recess Queen	2.93	Narrative	Change in font, type size, orientation, and color	O'Neill, A. (2002). *The recess queen*. New York: Scholastic.
The Worst Best Friend	3.52	Narrative	Change in type size and color	O'Neil, A. (2008). *The worst best friend*. New York: Scholastic.
Bobo and the New Neighbor	0.79	Narrative	Environmental print, change in font	Page, G. (2008). *Bobo and the new neighbor*. New York: Bloomsbury U.S.A. Children's Books.
Do You Do a Didgeridoo?	1.25	Narrative	Environmental print; change in font orientation and size	Page, N. (2008). *Do you do a didgeridoo?* Hertfordshire, UK: Make Believe Ideas.
Animal Action ABC	3.84	Informational	Change in font, type size, color, and orientation	Pandell, K. (1996). *Animal action ABC*. New York: Scholastic.
Ma! There's Nothing to Do Here!	2	Narrative	Change in type color and orientation; environmental print	Park, B. (2008). *Ma! There's nothing to do here!* New York: Random House.
Beethoven's Wig	0.9	Mixed	Environmental print; change in type color and orientation	Perlmutter, R. (2005). *Beethoven's wig*. Cambridge, MA: Rounder Books.
Ha, Ha, Baby!	0.76	Narrative	Change in type size	Petty, K. (2008). *Ha, ha, baby!* New York: Sterling.
Dog Breath	0.9	Narrative	Environmental print	Pilkey, D. (1994). *Dog breath*. New York: Scholastic.

Title	PSM	Genre	Interesting Features	Citation
Not a Box	0.19	Narrative	Environmental print	Portis, A. (2006). *Not a box*. New York: HarperCollins.
A Day in the Life of Murphy	0.87	Narrative	Environmental print	Provensen, A. (2003). *A day in the life of Murphy*. New York: Simon & Schuster Books for Young Readers.
Mouse Mess	0.85	Narrative	Environmental print	Riley, L. (1997). *Mouse mess*. New York: Blue Sky Press.
Rattletrap Car	1.72	Narrative	Change in type size and orientation	Root, P. (2001). *Rattletrap car*. Cambridge, MA: Candlewick Press.
We're Going on a Bear Hunt	0.47	Narrative	Change in type size	Rosen, M., & Oxenbury, H. (1989). *We're going on a bear hunt*. New York: Aladdin.
Cookies	1.57	Informational	Change in font and capitalization	Rosenthal, A. K. (2006). *Cookies*. New York: HarperCollins.
Meet Wild Boars	1.53	Narrative	Change in font size; environmental print	Rosoff, M. & Blackall, S. (2005). *Meet wild boars*. New York: Henry Holt.
The Squiggle	0.13	Narrative	Change in print location on page	Schaefer, C. L. (1996). *The squiggle*. New York: Crown.
Smash! Crash!	2.68	Narrative	Environmental print; change in type size and capitalization	Scieszka, J. (2008). *Smash! Crash!* New York: Simon & Schuster Books for Young Readers.
David Gets in Trouble	0.33	Narrative	Environmental print	Shannon, D. (2002). *David gets in trouble*. New York: Blue Sky Press.
Too Many Toys	1.23	Narrative	Change in capitalization, italic font	Shannon, D. (2008). *Too many toys*. New York: Blue Sky Press.
Dinosaur vs. Bedtime	1.63	Narrative	Change in font, capitalization, type color, and orientation	Shea, B. (2008). *Dinosaur vs. bedtime*. New York: Hyperion Books for Children.
Dogfish	1.52	Narrative	Change in font, type weight, capitalization	Shields, G. (2008). *Dogfish*. New York: Atheneum Books for Young Readers.
Wild about Books	2.1	Narrative	Environmental print	Sierra, J. (2004). *Wild about books*. New York: Knopf.

Title	PSM	Genre	Interesting Features	Citation
Miss Bindergarten Gets Ready for Kindergarten	3.88	Narrative	Change in font and type color; environmental print	Slate, J. (1996). *Miss Bindergarten gets ready for kindergarten.* New York: Dutton.
Clip-Clop	0.69	Narrative	Change in font	Smee, N. (2006). *Clip-clop.* New York: Boxer Books.
Ladybug Girl	1.61	Narrative	Change in type size and color	Soman, D. & Davis, J. (2008). *Ladybug girl.* New York: Dial Books for Young Readers.
Waking Up Wendell	1.31	Narrative	Environmental print	Stevens, A. & Hills, T. (2007). *Waking up Wendell.* New York: Schwartz & Wade Books.
Casey at the Bat	1.54	Narrative	Environmental print	Thayer, E. L. (2000). *Casey at the bat.* Brooklyn, NY: Handprint Books.
The Great Whitehouse Breakout	2.27	Narrative	Environmental print	Thomas, H. & Bok, C. (2008). *The great whitehouse breakout.* New York: Dial Books for Young Readers.
A Cold Winter's Good Knight	0.55	Narrative	Environmental print	Thomas, S. M. (2008). *A cold winter's good knight.* New York: Dutton Children's Books.
Somebody and the Three Blairs	0.08	Narrative	Italic font	Tolhurst, M. (1990). *Somebody and the three Blairs.* New York: Orchard Books.
There's a Dragon at My School	0.8	Narrative	Environmental print	Tyler, J., & Hawthorn, P. (1996). *There's a dragon at my school.* London: Usborne.
Duck at the Door	1.69	Narrative	Environmental print, change in font	Urbanovic, J. (2007). *Duck at the door.* New York: HarperCollins.
Duck Soup	1.52	Narrative	Change in type size and color	Urbanovic, J. (2008). *Duck soup.* New York: HarperCollins.
Jibberwillies at Night	3.69	Narrative	Change in type color, size, and orientation	Vail, R. (2008). *Jibberwillies at night.* New York: Scholastic Press.
There Was a Coyote Who Swallowed a Flea	0.66	Narrative	Environmental print, italic font	Ward, J. (2007). *There was a coyote who swallowed a flea.* New York: Rising Moon.
The Nicest Naughty Fairy	2.38	Narrative	Change in type size and capitalization; environmental print	Ward, N. (2008). *The nicest naughty fairy.* London: Meadowside Children's Books.

Title	PSM	Genre	Interesting Features	Citation
Bunny Cakes	0.95	Narrative	Environmental print	Wells, R. (1997). *Bunny cakes.* New York: Scholastic.
Knuffle Bunny	0.81	Narrative	Environmental print	Willems, M. (2004). *Knuffle bunny.* New York: Hyperion Books for Children.
Leonardo the Terrible Monster	0.8	Narrative	Change in type color	Willems, M. (2005). *Leonardo the terrible monster.* New York: Hyperion Books for Children.
More More More Said the Baby	0.21	Narrative	Change in type size	Williams, V. B. (1990). *More, more, more, said the baby.* New York: Greenwillow Books.
The Night before Kindergarten	0.07	Narrative	Environmental print	Wing, N. (2001). *The night before kindergarten.* New York: Grosset & Dunlap.
Jake Starts School	1.5	Narrative	Environmental print	Wright, M. (2008). *Jake starts school.* New York: Feiwel and Friends.
Is There a Mouse in the Baby's Room?	0.43	Narrative	Environmental print	Zechel, E. (2008). *Is there a mouse in the baby's room?* New York: Lark Books.

Scope and Sequence of Storybooks for 30-Week Reading Program with Print-Knowledge Objectives Tracking Sheet

Week	Book Title	Print-Knowledge Objectives
1	*My First Day of School*	Environmental print Concept of reading
2	*There's a Dragon at My School*	Print direction Concept of words in print
3	*I Like It When …*	Author of book Function of print
4	*The Dandelion Seed*	Upper- and lower-case forms Page organization
5	*Down by the Cool of the Pool*	Title of book Word identification
6	*More More More, said the Baby*	Concept of letter Page organization
7	*Jamboree Day*	Page order Letter names
8	*Rumble in the Jungle*	Word identification Concept of letter
9	*David Gets in Trouble*	Author of book Letters and words

Week	Book Title	Print-Knowledge Objectives
10	*The Way I Feel*	Short words and long words Function of print
11	*Spot Bakes a Cake*	Concept of letter Environmental print
12	*We're Going on a Bear Hunt*	Upper- and lower-case forms Page order
13	*Dear Mr. Blueberry*	Title of book Function of print
14	*Growing Vegetable Soup*	Page organization Short words and long words
15	*Froggy Gets Dressed*	Letter names Concept of reading
16	*I Stink!*	Concept of letter Page order
17	*Animal Action ABC*	Letters and words Letter names
18	*My Backpack*	Upper- and lower-case forms Concept of word in print
19	*Baghead*	Short words and long words Print direction
20	*A Color of His Own*	Page organization Concept of reading
21	*To Market, to Market*	Word identification Print direction
22	*Hey, Little Ant*	Title of book Upper- and lower-case forms
23	*Mouse Mess*	Environmental print Page order
24	*In the Small, Small Pond*	Concept of words in print Print direction
25	*The Grumpy Morning*	Letter names Concept of reading

Week	Book Title	Print-Knowledge Objectives
26	*The Noisy Airplane Ride*	Letters and words Function of print
27	*How to Speak Moo!*	Title of book Word identification
28	*Never Spit on Your Shoes*	Author of book Environmental print
29	*The Recess Queen*	Short words and long words Author of book
30	*Miss Bindergarten Gets Ready for Kindergarten*	Concept of word in print Letters and words

Print-Knowledge Objectives Tracking Sheet

Month: _____

	Week:	Week:	Week:	Week:
Book and Print Organization				
Title of book				
Author of book				
Page order				
Page organization				
Print direction				
Print Meaning				
Function of print				
Environmental print				
Concept of reading				
Letters				
Upper- and lower-case forms				
Letter names				
Concept of letter				
Words				
Concept of words in print				
Short words and long words				
Letters and words				
Word identification				

STAR Target Cards for 30-Week Reading Program

Book Title

TARGET:

★ High-Support Examples

TECHNIQUE:

TECHNIQUE:

★ Low-Support Examples

TECHNIQUE:

TECHNIQUE:

STAR: Sit Together and Read

My First Day of School

TARGET: Environmental Print

★ High-Support Examples

1) TECHNIQUE: MODELING THE ANSWER

   Teacher: We see words and letters at the bottom of this page. Who can show me where we see words and letters somewhere else?

   Child: Here? (*Points to tray of food.*)

   Teacher: Almost. Here, here are some letters and words on the cereal box. (*Reads Snappy Snax, then moves to calendar and bread bag.*)

2) TECHNIQUE: ELICITING THE ANSWER

   Teacher: This sign says "Safety First!" Can anyone tell me what this sign says?

   Child: Safety First!

   Teacher: That is exactly right! The sign says "Safety First."

★ Low-Support Examples

1) TECHNIQUE: ENCOURAGEMENT

   Teacher: Who can find the *W* on this page? William, I think you can find it since you know how to spell your name.

   William: Up here?

   Teacher: You got it! That is the letter *W*, just like in *William* and *Wanda*.

2) TECHNIQUE: EXPLANATION

   Teacher: Can anyone read what this sign says?

   Child: *Stop*!

   Teacher: You knew that! Yes, this sign says *Stop*. You see this sign on the road when you are riding in the car.

STAR: Sit Together and Read

My First Day of School

TARGET: Concept of Reading

★ High-Support Examples

1) TECHNIQUE: MODELING THE ANSWER

Teacher: This book is called *My First Day of School*. I can't wait to read this book. I think we are going to learn about being at school on the first day, and maybe about meeting new friends, too. What else are we going to learn?

Child: Look at the pictures of the boy!

Teacher: We will look at pictures of the boy, and we're going to *read* it, and learn all kinds of things about school and being there on the first day. You guys know all about this, but now we'll read about it, too.

2) TECHNIQUE: ELICITING THE ANSWER

Teacher: This book is titled *My First Day of School*. This book is about things that happen on the first day of school. What do you think this story is about?

Child: Riding a bus!

Teacher: I think you're right. Riding a bus is something many of you do on the first day of school. I think we'll learn other things about the first day, too.

★ Low-Support Examples

1) TECHNIQUE: PREDICTION

Teacher: Today we're going to read this book. Look at the cover. What do you think we'll learn from reading this book?

Child: About school?

Teacher: Yes, I think so too. We'll learn about things that happen at school.

2) TECHNIQUE: RELATING TO THE CHILD'S EXPERIENCE

Teacher: Let's look at this picture. I think these must look familiar to you. Can anyone tell us what this page teaches us?

Child: It looks like the place where I put my stuff.

Teacher: Exactly. I think this page will remind us to keep things neat and clean in our room.

STAR: Sit Together and Read

There's a Dragon at My School

TARGET: Print Direction

★ High-Support Examples

1) TECHNIQUE: REDUCING CHOICES/GIVING ALTERNATIVES

Teacher: Where should we start reading on this page? Here (*points to first word on the page*) or here (*points to last word on the page*)?

Child: Here! (*Points to first word.*)

Teacher: Yes, that's right. We begin reading here and we finish here. (*Runs finger along text.*)

2) TECHNIQUE: ELICITING THE ANSWER

Teacher: I start reading here. Who can show me where I start reading?

Child: Here?

Teacher: That is exactly right. I start right here, where the first word is, and I go this way. (*Runs finger along top line.*)

★ Low-Support Examples

1) TECHNIQUE: EXPLANATION

Teacher: Where do I start reading?

Child: Here!

Teacher: Right. Remember, we always start reading here and stop reading here.

2) TECHNIQUE: ENCOURAGEMENT

Teacher: Samantha, can you show me which way I should read this page? I bet you know this —you showed me last time.

Child: This way. (*Runs finger in correct direction.*)

Teacher: I knew you would remember. Good job! We read this way, just like Samantha showed us.

STAR: Sit Together and Read

There's a Dragon at My School

TARGET: Concept of Words in Print

★ High-Support Examples

1) TECHNIQUE: ELICITING THE ANSWER

Teacher: This is the word *plunk* right here. What is this word?

Children: *Plunk*!

Teacher: Wonderful! Yes, this word says *plunk*.

2) TECHNIQUE: COPARTICIPATION

Teacher: This is the title of the book. It is made up of words. Let's count how many words are in the title. Count with me while I point. (*Begins counting.*)

Child: 1-2-3-4-5-6.

Teacher: You got it! There are six words in the title.

★ Low-Support Examples

1) TECHNIQUE: EXPLANATION

Teacher: Is this a word? (*Points to picture of boy on cover.*)

Child: No! That's a boy, not a word.

Teacher: Yep, that is a picture of a boy. This is a word. (*Points to a word.*)

2) TECHNIQUE: PREDICTION

Teacher: What word do you think we might find on this page.

Child: *Dragon*!

Teacher: I do see the word *dragon*. It's right here.

STAR: Sit Together and Read

I Like It When . . .

TARGET: Author of Book

★ High-Support Examples

1) TECHNIQUE: MODELING THE ANSWER

Teacher: What does an author do? Remember, we talked about the difference between an author and an illustrator. The illustrator draws the pictures, so what must the author do?

Child: Draw pictures?

Teacher: Not quite, the author is the person who writes the book. The author of this book is Mary Murphy. We see her name right here.

2) TECHNIQUE: COPARTICIPATION

Teacher: These words are the author's name. They say *Mary Murphy*. Senica, come up and point to the author's name for us.

Child: Where is the name?

Teacher: Here, give me your finger. There you go—that says *Mary Murphy*. She's the author of the book.

★ Low-Support Examples

1) TECHNIQUE: EXPLANATION

Teacher: Whose name is on the front of this book?

Child: The author's!

Teacher: That's right! The name *Mary Murphy* is on the front of this book because she wrote the book. Great job!

2) TECHNIQUE: ENCOURAGEMENT

Teacher: Why do you think this name is on the front of the book? Johnny, I bet you know why—you knew last time!

Child: Because they wrote the book!

Teacher: You're right! The author wrote the book, and so her name is on the front.

STAR: Sit Together and Read

I Like It When . . .

TARGET: Function of Print

★ High-Support Examples

1) TECHNIQUE: ELICITING THE ANSWER

   Teacher: This is where the penguin is talking. Show me where the penguin is talking.

   Child: Right here.

   Teacher: That's right! Those are the penguin's words!

2) TECHNIQUE: REDUCING CHOICES/GIVING ALTERNATIVES

   Teacher: Is the baby penguin talking here (*points to the word bubble saying* boo) or here (*points to the momma penguin*)?

   Child: Um, here? (*Points to the momma penguin.*)

   Teacher: The baby penguin's words are here. (*Points to word bubble.*)

★ Low-Support Examples

1) TECHNIQUE: PREDICTION

   Teacher: What do you think the words in this bubble mean?

   Child: That the baby wants to say something?

   Teacher: That's right! The baby is surprising its mom, and it says *boo*!

2) TECHNIQUE: EXPLANATION

   Teacher: Can you show me where the momma penguin is talking?

   Child: Here?

   Teacher: That's right! We know the momma penguin is talking because she has a speech bubble over her head.

STAR: Sit Together and Read

The Dandelion Seed

TARGET: Upper- and Lower-Case Forms

★ High-Support Examples

1) TECHNIQUE: COPARTICIPATION

Teacher: This is an upper-case letter.

Child: Where?

Teacher: Here, give me your finger. (*Takes child's finger and places it on an upper-case letter.*) This is an upper-case letter. It is an upper-case T.

2) TECHNIQUE: REDUCING CHOICES/GIVING ALTERNATIVES

Teacher: Which one is an upper-case letter? This one (*points to an upper-case* D) or this one (*points to a lower-case* c)?

Child: (*Points to* c.)

Teacher: That one is a lower-case *c*. This is an upper-case letter. This is an upper-case *D*.

★ Low-Support Examples

1) TECHNIQUE: RELATING TO THE CHILD'S EXPERIENCE

Teacher: What upper-case letter is this? Billy, I bet you know, because you have this letter in your name!

Child: *B*!

Teacher: That's right! It's a *B*.

2) TECHNIQUE: EXPLANATION

Teacher: Can you point to one upper-case letter?

Child: Um, this one?

Teacher: That's right! This *O* is an upper-case letter. It is bigger than all the other letters.

STAR: Sit Together and Read

The Dandelion Seed

TARGET: Page Organization

★ High-Support Examples

1) TECHNIQUE: MODELING THE ANSWER

Teacher: Now let's think about where the top of our page is. I know that this is the bottom, so the top must be where?

Child: Right here. (*Points to middle of page at picture.*)

Teacher: Almost—this is the top of the page. This is where I start reading. (*Points to printed text.*)

2) TECHNIQUE: REDUCING CHOICES/GIVING ALTERNATIVES

Teacher: Is this the top of the page (*points to the bottom of the page*) or is this the top of the page (*points to the top of the page*)?

Child: Um, here? (*Points to the bottom of the page.*)

Teacher: That's the bottom of the page. This is the top of the page. This is where I start reading.

★ Low-Support Examples

1) TECHNIQUE: ENCOURAGEMENT

Teacher: Where do you think the top of the page is? Spencer, I know you'll know this because you knew it before!

Child: Right here?

Teacher: That's right! Everyone look where Spencer pointed. Right here is the top of the page.

2) TECHNIQUE: EXPLANATION

Teacher: Can you show me the top of the page?

Child: Here?

Teacher: That's right! The top of the page is right here, and that's where we find the words to start reading!

STAR: Sit Together and Read

Down by the Cool of the Pool

TARGET: Title of Book

★ High-Support Examples

1) TECHNIQUE: ELICITING THE ANSWER

Teacher: This is the name of the book. It says *Down by the Cool of the Pool*. What is the name of the book?

Child: *Down by the Cool of the Pool*!

Teacher: You got it!

2) TECHNIQUE: COPARTICIPATION

Teacher: We can find the name of the book on the front cover. Let's point to it together, Amy!

Child: (*Points to title with teacher.*)

Teacher: Good job. We just pointed to the title of our book.

★ Low-Support Examples

1) TECHNIQUE: EXPLANATION

Teacher: What are the words on the front of the book called?

Child: Its name?

Teacher: That's right! The words on the front of the book tell us the title of the book. The title is the name of the book. The title of this book is *Down by the Cool of the Pool*.

2) TECHNIQUE: ENCOURAGEMENT

Teacher: Who can show me the title of this book? Patrick, you'll know this, because you've read this book many times, and we've talked about it together.

Child: Right here!

Teacher: Exactly right! This is our title.

STAR: Sit Together and Read

Down by the Cool of the Pool

TARGET: Word Identification

★ High-Support Examples

1) TECHNIQUE: COPARTICIPATION

Teacher: This word says *wheee*. I'll point to it and let's say it together! I bet we'll see this word again! Remember what it looks like so you can help me read it on the next pages!

Teacher and Children: *Wheee!*

Teacher: That is a fun word to say! Yes, this word is *wheee*.

2) TECHNIQUE: ELICITING THE ANSWER

Teacher: This word is *pool*. What is this word?

Child: *Pool!*

Teacher: Great job! This word says *pool!*

★ Low-Support Examples

1) TECHNIQUE: EXPLANATION

Teacher: What sound does water make when you jump into the pool?

Child: Splash!

Teacher: That's right! And this is the word *splash*. We see it because the animals all fell into the pool!

2) TECHNIQUE: RELATING TO THE CHILD'S EXPERIENCE

Teacher: What word do you think this is? (*Points to the word* cat.) Ashley, I bet you know this word because you have this as a pet!

Child: A kitty!

Teacher: Almost! This word says *cat*. It is spelled *c-a-t*.

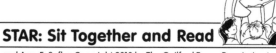

STAR: Sit Together and Read

"More More More" Said the Baby

TARGET: Concept of Letter

★ High-Support Examples

1) TECHNIQUE: COPARTICIPATION

Teacher: This letter is *M*. We see this letter in lots of words. We see M in the word *More* and in the word *pumpkin*. Let's point to all the letter *M*'s on this page, Anita.

Child: (*Points to M's.*)

Teacher: And this is the letter *M*, too. And here is another letter *M*.

2) TECHNIQUE: MODELING THE ANSWER

Teacher: The letter *L* is in this word (points to *Little*) and this word (points to *like*). And I know there are two *L*'s in your name, Lionel. Does that mean I can use the letter *L* in other words?

Child: Yes?

Teacher: That's right! We see the letter *L* in lots of words, like *laugh* and *lunch*.

★ Low-Support Examples

1) TECHNIQUE: RELATING TO THE CHILD'S EXPERIENCE

Teacher: The word *baby* has two *b*'s in it. Can you think of another word that has the letter *b* in it? Bobby, I bet you'll be able to!

Child: *Bobby*!

Teacher: That's right! Your name has three *b*'s in it!

2) TECHNIQUE: EXPLANATION

Teacher: Can you point to three *T*'s on this page?

Child: (*Points to the T's.*)

Teacher: That's right! This is the letter *T*! We see this letter in lots of different words. In fact, every letter we know in the alphabet is used to make all kinds of different words.

STAR: Sit Together and Read

"More More More," Said the Baby

TARGET: Page organization

★ High-Support Examples

1) TECHNIQUE: ELICITING THE ANSWER

Teacher: This is the top of the page. Can you show me the top of the page?

Child: Here? (*Points to top of page.*)

Teacher: Right! This is where I start reading.

2) TECHNIQUE: COPARTICIPATION

Teacher: This is the top of the page.

Child: Where?

Teacher: Right here. Cooper, point to the top of the page with me and we'll all say *top* when we point!

Child: (*Points to the top of the page.*)

Teacher: Excellent! Let's say *top* together since this is the top of the page.

★ Low-Support Examples

1) TECHNIQUE: ENCOURAGEMENT

Teacher: Where do you think the top of the page is? Austin, I know you'll know this because you showed me this morning when you were looking at the book.

Child: Right here?

Teacher: That's right!

2) TECHNIQUE: EXPLANATION

Teacher: Can you show me the top of the page?

Child: Here?

Teacher: That's right! The top of the page is right here. This is a good place to look for words to start reading.

STAR: Sit Together and Read

Jamboree Day

TARGET: Page Order

★ High-Support Examples

1) TECHNIQUE: MODELING THE ANSWER

Teacher: I'm trying to figure out where I should start reading. When I've read you stories before, I always start here (*points to left page*). Where should I start reading this time?

Child: Here? (*Points to right page.*)

Teacher: Not there. If I did that, I might get lost in the story. I need to start reading on this page, then I read that page next!

2) TECHNIQUE: ELICITING THE ANSWER

Teacher: I start reading on this page. Can you show me the page where I start reading?

Child: Here!

Teacher: You got it. I start reading right where Preston pointed.

★ Low-Support Examples

1) TECHNIQUE: EXPLANATION

Teacher: Can you show me which page I read first and which page I read last?

Child: This one and this one?

Teacher: That's right! I read this page first. Then I turn the pages this way and read this page last!

2) TECHNIQUE: ENCOURAGEMENT

Teacher: Who can show me which way I turn the pages when I read? Alice, I bet you can—I saw you turning the pages in your book during center time!

Child: This way?

Teacher: That's right! This is the way you turn the pages. Very good.

STAR: Sit Together and Read

Jamboree Day

TARGET: Letter Names

★ High-Support Examples

1) TECHNIQUE: ELICITING THE ANSWER

Teacher: This letter is a *D*. Can you show me the letter *D*?

Child: Here? (*Points to an* L.)

Teacher: That's an *L*, not a *D*. This is the letter *D*.

2) TECHNIQUE: REDUCING CHOICES/GIVING ALTERNATIVES

Teacher: Is this the letter *J* (*points to the letter* D) or is this the letter *J* (*points to the* J)?

Child: This one?

Teacher: That's right! This is the letter *J*. It's the first letter in the word *Jamboree*.

★ Low-Support Examples

1) TECHNIQUE: RELATING TO THE CHILD'S EXPERIENCE

Teacher: What letter is this? David knows. His name starts with the same letter!

Child: *D*!

Teacher: That's right! This is the letter *D*, like in *David*.

2) TECHNIQUE: EXPLANATIONS

Teacher: Can you show me the letter *J*?

Child: Here?

Teacher: That's right! The letter *J* is the first letter in the word *Jamboree*.

STAR: Sit Together and Read

Rumble in the Jungle

TARGET: Word Identification

★ High-Support Examples

1) TECHNIQUE: COPARTICIPATION

   Teacher: This word is *Jungle.*

   Child: Where?

   Teacher: Here, let's point to it together. This word says *Jungle.*

2) TECHNIQUE: ELICITING THE ANSWER

   Teacher: This word says *crocodile.* What word is it?

   Child: *Crocodile!*

   Teacher: *Crocodile*, yes! He looks a little scary.

★ Low-Support Examples

1) TECHNIQUE: EXPLANATION

   Teacher: Is this word *snake* or *giraffe?*

   Child: Um, *snake?*

   Teacher: That's right! We know that says *snake* because there's a picture of a snake next to it.

2) TECHNIQUE: PREDICTION

   Teacher: What kinds of words do you think we'll see in this book?

   Child: I think we'll see names of animals, because there are animals on the front of the book!

   Teacher: Let's see, I see lots of words about animals. This word is *lion* and this word is *tiger.*

STAR: Sit Together and Read

Rumble in the Jungle

TARGET: Concept of Letter

★ High-Support Examples

1) TECHNIQUE: MODELING THE ANSWER

Teacher: The letters *l*, *i*, *o*, and *n* make the word *lion*.

Child: Here? (*Points to* Jungle.)

Teacher: Excellent! Here is the *l* in *Rumble* and the *l* in *Jungle*.

2) TECHNIQUE: ELICITING THE ANSWER

Teacher: Letters make up words. What do letters do?

Child: Make up words?

Teacher: That's right! Letters make up words!

★ Low-Support Examples

1) TECHNIQUE: RELATING TO THE CHILD'S EXPERIENCE

Teacher: The word *Jungle* starts with the letter *J*. Jacob knows this because it's the first letter in his name. What other words do you know that start with the letter *J*? Jason?

Child: My name, too!

Teacher: Of course! *Jason* and *Jacob* both start with the letter *J*.

2) TECHNIQUE: EXPLANATION

Teacher: Does anyone know what words are made of?

Child: Letters?

Teacher: That's right! Words are made of lots of different letters. And you will see that the same letter can be used to make up different words, like *c* is in *cat* and *c* is also in *cart*.

STAR: Sit Together and Read

David Gets in Trouble

TARGET: Author of Book

★ High-Support Examples

1) TECHNIQUE: ELICITING THE ANSWER

Teacher: The person who wrote the book is called the *author*. His name is right here. Who can point to the author's name?

Child: Here?

Teacher: Almost—that's the title of the book. Here is the author's name. His name is *David Shannon*.

2) TECHNIQUE: COPARTICIPATION

Teacher: Let's look at the name on this page. This name is *David Shannon*. It's the name of the author. Let's all say *author* together.

Teacher and Children: *Author!*

Teacher: Yes, David Shannon is the author, and his name is right here.

★ Low-Support Examples

1) TECHNIQUE: EXPLANATION

Teacher: Whose name is on the front of the book?

Child: The author's!

Teacher: That's right! The author's name is on the front of the book because he wrote the book!

2) TECHNIQUE: RELATING TO THE CHILD'S EXPERIENCE

Teacher: Can anyone tell me the name on the front of the book? David, I bet you'll know this because he has the same name!

Child: David!

Teacher: You are right! You and the author, David, share the same first name.

STAR: Sit Together and Read

David Gets in Trouble

TARGET: Letters and Words

★ High-Support Examples

1) TECHNIQUE: COPARTICIPATION

Teacher: This page has three words on it, *I was hungry.* Let's count the words while I point. (*After pointing to the words, counts the total number of letters in each word.*)

Teacher and Children: 1-2-3.

Teacher: Wonderful—three words are on this page. Now let's count each letter in the word *hungry.*

Teacher and Children: 1-2-3-4-5-6.

Teacher: Very good. Six letters in our word *hungry.* How many letters are in the word *hungry?*

Children: Six!

Teacher: Yes, six letters are in the word *hungry.*

2) TECHNIQUE: ELICITING THE ANSWER

Teacher: This page has five words on it. Does this page have five words or five letters on it?

Child: Letters?

Teacher: Almost—this page has five *words* on it. Let's count them: 1-2-3-4-5. Now let's count the letters in the words. We're going to find that there are many more letters since they make up the words. (*Begins counting the letters.*)

★ Low-Support Examples

1) TECHNIQUE: EXPLANATION

Teacher: How many letters are in the word *dog?*

Child: Three?

Teacher: That's right! There are three letters in the word *dog: d-o-g.*

2) TECHNIQUE: ENCOURAGEMENT

Teacher: How many letters are in the word *excuse?* Chris, I bet you'll know this, we counted letters yesterday.

Child: 1-2-3-4-5-6.

Teacher: Good job! Those six letters make up the word *excuse.*

STAR: Sit Together and Read

The Way I Feel

TARGET: Short Words and Long Words

★ High-Support Examples

1) TECHNIQUE: REDUCING CHOICES/GIVING ALTERNATIVES

Teacher: Look at these two words. Which word do you think is a short word—this word (*points to* thunder) or this word (*points to* the)?

Child: (*Points to* the.)

Teacher: You are exactly right. The word *the* is a short word. It has only three letters in it. *Thunder* is a long word—it has seven letters in it. (*Counts letters with finger.*)

2) TECHNIQUE: MODELING

Teacher: Look at this boy. It looks like he's jumping up and down! This word (*points to* excited) is a long word. It has (*begins counting*) seven letters in it. Is *excited* a long word or a short word, do you think?

Children: Long word!

Teacher: *Excited* is a long word with seven letters in it. Let's look back at the word *sad*. *Sad* is a short word with only three letters in it.

★ Low-Support Examples

1) TECHNIQUE: EXPLANATION

Teacher: Who can point to the longest word on this page?

Child: (*Points to* scared *at the bottom of the page.*)

Teacher: Oooo, that is a long word—it has (*begins counting*) six letters in it. We see the word here, too (*points to the word in the sentence*). I'm going to count the letters in another word to see if it is shorter or longer than *scared* just to make sure. I think I'll count the letters in this word *lightning*. (*Begins counting the letters in* lightning.) This looks like a long word. It has nine letters in it! Three more than *scared*! That means that *lightning* is longer than *scared*. But only by a little bit!

2) TECHNIQUE: PREDICTION

Teacher: Let's look at this page. This is the word *sad*. Do you think *sad* will be one of the shortest words on the page or one of the longest words on the page?

Child: Shortest!

Teacher: Yep, we know that because it only has three letters in it. Lots of words have more than three letters in them.

STAR: Sit Together and Read

The Way I Feel

TARGET: Function of Print

★ High-Support Examples

1) TECHNIQUE: ELICITING ANSWER

Teacher: Oh, my. Look at this word! This word is *silly*. Look at the shapes of the letters. Squiggly, colorful, and look at the eyes! They really look silly, don't they? This word looks like what it means, doesn't it? It says *silly*. What is this word?

Child: *Silly!*

Teacher: It is *silly!*

2) TECHNIQUE: MODELING

Teacher: Why in the world is this word all thick and dark with jagged edges? When I see a word that looks like that, I think it might be the word *angry*. It's all pointy and sharp. What do you think this word is trying to tell us?

Child: It's big!

Teacher: It is big. And the dark letters and jagged edges give us a clue to what the word is. The word is *angry*. We can tell by the way it is written! The little boy on this page is *angry*.

★ Low-Support Examples

1) TECHNIQUE: RELATING TO THE CHILD'S EXPERIENCE

Teacher: Look at this boy. He looks very, very happy. And look at this word. It looks like it's jumping up and down, too. And it's all swirly and colorful. How do you feel when you feel swirly and colorful?

Children: (*Work through answers of* happy, surprised, *until they get to* excited.)

Teacher: Yes! When you look at the word *excited* like it is written here, you think of being excited!

2) TECHNIQUE: PREDICTIONS

Teacher: How do you think this boy feels? Does the way this word is written make you think of how he feels?

Children: (*Work through answers of* happy, surprised, *until they get to* excited.)

Teacher: I think he is excited, too. I think he's more than happy since the letters in the word *excited* seem to be jumping off the page!

STAR: Sit Together and Read

Spot Bakes a Cake

TARGET: Concept of Letter

★ High-Support Examples

1) TECHNIQUE: ELICITING THE ANSWER

Teacher: Take a look at this page. This sentence reads, "Now we can make the cake." I see the letter a many times (*points to the words with* a *in them*). Can someone point to all the words with the letter *a* in them?

Child: (*Points to all the words.*)

Teacher: (*Opens flap on the page.*) Surprise! Here are even more words than all the ones you found with the letter *a* in them (*points to* already *and* started). The letter *a* sure does help make a lot of words on these pages!

2) TECHNIQUE: COPARTICIPATION

Teacher: This word says *Spot.* He is a character in our book. *Spot* has the letter *o* in it, right here. Make the shape of the letter *o* with your finger.

Teacher and Children: (*Make shape of the letter* o *in the air.*)

Teacher: Excellent! The letter *o* is round like a circle. It is right here in *Spot.*

★ Low-Support Examples

1) TECHNIQUE: ENCOURAGEMENT

Teacher: When we read *Rumble in the Jungle*, we talked about how the same letter can be seen in many different words. We're going to do that again with *Spot Bakes a Cake*. I was so pleased how well you all did at spotting the same letter in different words. Beth, why don't you point to all the words with the letter *o* in them? We can all help you if you get stuck.

Child: (*Points to the words.*)

Teacher: I knew you could do it! *On* and *Spot* have the letter *o* in them.

2) TECHNIQUE: EXPLANATION

Teacher: Can anyone point to all the words with the letter *d* in them?

Child: (*Points to all the words.*)

Teacher: You did that very well. All of these words have the letter *d* in them, even though they are very different words. (*Reads over the words while pointing to the letter* d.)

STAR: Sit Together and Read

Spot Bakes a Cake

TARGET: Function of Print

★ High-Support Examples

1) TECHNIQUE: ELICITING THE ANSWER

Teacher: We can tell that Spot is saying something because we see this bubble by his mouth. He is saying "Let's bake a cake!" Yum! Who can show me where Spot is saying "Let's bake a cake!"?

Child: (*Points to the speech bubble.*)

Teacher: Yep, you got it. We know this is something Spot is saying.

2) TECHNIQUE: REDUCING CHOICES/GIVING ALTERNATIVES

Teacher: Who is saying *Wheee*! on these pages? Is it the mother dog or is it the mouse?

Child: Mouse!

Teacher: Very good. You knew that because of the speech bubble right here and this line that points right to the mouse.

★ Low-Support Examples

1) TECHNIQUE: RELATING TO THE CHILD'S EXPERIENCE

Teacher: How many of you remember making birthday cards for people in your family? It looks like Spot is doing the same thing for his dad. Can someone point to what Spot has written on the card for this dad?

Child: He wrote this to his dad, like I did.

Teacher: Oh, that is interesting. Yes, this is where Spot wrote on the card he made.

2) TECHNIQUE: EXPLANATION

Teacher: Who can point to the words that Spot is saying? This is a tricky one since there is no bubble to help you.

Child: (*Points to the larger text on top of the page.*)

Teacher: This is a tricky one. You pointed to a question the father dog is asking. He is asking, "Did you make the cake, Spot?" And then he says, "It's delicious!" We know what Spot is saying because the words are closest to him. Spot is saying, "Thanks, Dad. Mom helped a little." See how close these words are to where Spot is on the page? That's how we know they are for him.

STAR: Sit Together and Read

We're Going on a Bear hunt

TARGET: Upper- and Lower-Case Forms

★ High-Support Examples

1) TECHNIQUE: REDUCE CHOICES/GIVING ALTERNATIVES

Teacher: It looks like the family has to go through long grass to get where they're going! Let's read the bottom of this page, "Oh no! We've got to go through it!" Which is the upper-case *O*, this one or this one (*points to the letter* O *in both* Oh *and in* no).

Child: (*Points at the* O *in* Oh.)

Teacher: Exactly. Upper-case means that we look for the big letter, like the big *O* in *Oh.*

2) TECHNIQUE: COPARTICIPATION

Teacher: OK now. I'm going to point to the upper-case *T* in *Tiptoe* (*points to letter*) and to the lower-case *t* in *Tiptoe* (*points to letter*). When I point, I want all of you to call out *upper case* or *lower case*.

Children: Upper case! (*Teacher points to the* T *in* Tiptoe.)

Teacher: Right! Upper-case *T* in *Tiptoe.*

★ Low-Support Examples

1) TECHNIQUE: ENCOURAGEMENT

Teacher: Let's look at this sentence. It says, "Back through the river! Splash splosh! Splash splosh! Splash splosh!" Those are silly words, aren't they? I'll bet Sean can show us the upper-case *S*'s in this sentence.

Child: In my name, right here.

Teacher: Yes, there is an upper-case *S*, just like in your name, Sean.

2) TECHNIQUE: EXPLANATION

Teacher: Tonya, can you show me where the upper-case *B* is in this sentence? It says, "Back upstairs."

Child: It's here (*points to* B).

Teacher: Very good. Look at the upper-case *B* and now look at this *b* (*points to* bedroom). It's different, isn't it? One is a big *B*, the other is the little *b*. They have different shapes.

STAR: Sit Together and Read

We're Going on a Bear Hunt

TARGET: Page Order

★ High-Support Examples

1) TECHNIQUE: ELICITING THE ANSWER

Teacher: I am going to turn the pages this way (*shows how pages are turned from left to right*) so that I understand what is happening. Now you show me which way we turn the pages so that we can read this story.

Child: (*Begins turning the pages left to right.*)

Teacher: Wonderful! That is exactly right, you turn the pages left to right.

2) TECHNIQUE: COPARTICIPATION

Teacher: Jamal, why don't you come up here and turn the pages of *We're Going on a Bear Hunt* while I read it to everyone. I'll help you.

Child: (*Begins turning pages all at once.*)

Teacher: Whoops! Wait until I finish reading the page before you turn it! You did a great job turning them the right way.

★ Low-Support Examples

1) TECHNIQUE: ENCOURAGEMENT

Teacher: Laura, you helped me turn the pages of the story we read last week. I think you are ready to do this all by yourself. Why don't you come up and hold the book and turn the pages while I read it?

Child: (*Turns pages correctly.*)

Teacher: You are doing a wonderful job turning the pages the right way.

2) TECHNIQUE: PREDICTION

Teacher: Here I am on the first page of the story. If I want to sneak to the end of the book to see the last page, which way do I turn the pages?

Child: This way to peek. (*Turns pages to the end to the end of the book.*)

Teacher: That is exactly how I can peek at the end of the book—just like you turned the pages.

STAR: Sit Together and Read

Dear Mr. Blueberry

TARGET: Title of Book

★ High-Support Examples

1) TECHNIQUE: REDUCING CHOICES/GIVING ALTERNATIVES

Teacher: Today we are going to read this book. We find the title of the book on the cover. Which one do you think is the title? This (*points to title*) or this (*points to picture in right corner*)?

Child: (*Points to the title.*)

Teacher: Good job! Yes, that is the title, and it tells us the name of the book, *Dear Mr. Blueberry.*

2) TECHNIQUE: ELICITING THE ANSWER

Teacher: Today we are going to read *Dear Mr. Blueberry.* The title is right here (*points to title*) on the cover. Who can show me where the title is?

Child: Is this part of the title (*points to author's name*)?

Teacher: That is a little confusing since it is so close to the title. The title is here—it is *Dear Mr. Blueberry.* You pointed to the author's name. Remember we talked about the author before? The author of this book is Simon James. It says it here. It is in a different place than the title.

★ Low-Support Examples

1) TECHNIQUE: ENCOURAGEMENT

Teacher: We are going to read this book called *Dear Mr. Blueberry.* We've done a lot of reading since we started school, and I think someone can come up here and point to the title for us. LaTisha, come on up and show us where the title is.

Child: This is the title. (*Points to one word in the title.*)

Teacher: Very good. *Dear* is part of the title. This is the whole title of our book—three words, *Dear Mr. Blueberry.* (*Points to each word of the title, then runs finger along it.*)

2) TECHNIQUE: EXPLANATION

Teacher: Can anyone point to the title of the book for us?

Child: (*Points to title.*)

Teacher: Excellent! And that was a little tricky, since the author's name (*points to it*) is right below the title. But we can tell it's the title since these letters look like someone wrote them, like name is a little bit smaller. Good job.

STAR: Sit Together and Read

Dear Mr. Blueberry

TARGET: Function of Print

★ High-Support Examples

1) TECHNIQUE: MODELING THE ANSWER

Teacher: The cover of this book looks like something the mailman might deliver to us, like a letter. These words look like somebody actually did write them on the cover. Can anyone tell me what the cover of this book looks like? Does it remind you of something you get in the mail?

Child: I get presents!

Teacher: I love to get presents in the mail, too. And with your presents you probably also get a … letter! See how this looks like the stamp, and this looks like someone's handwriting? And here we see where the letter is from. The post office puts this kind of stamp on all letters and packages. This cover looks like a letter or a package.

2) TECHNIQUE: REDUCING CHOICES/GIVING ALTERNATIVES

Teacher: When somebody writes *Dear Caroline,* or *Dear Zachary,* or *Dear Mr. Blueberry,* the title of our book, what are they going to write to Caroline, Zachary, or Mr. Blueberry? Are they going to write a shopping list like the ones you write in housekeeping, or does it sound like they are going to write a letter?

Children: Letter!

Teacher: Exactly. The way the title of the book is written, it looks like we'll be reading letters to Mr. Blueberry.

★ Low-Support Examples

1) TECHNIQUE: EXPLANATION

Teacher: Let's take a look at the first page of our story. Can anyone tell me what this looks like (*traces finger over the lines of the letter*)? It looks like someone signed the bottom of it.

Child: It's a letter!

Teacher: It does look like a letter. It begins with *Dear Mr. Blueberry,* and Emily has signed the letter *Love, Emily.* That's how you would sign a note to someone in your family, isn't it?

2) TECHNIQUE: RELATING TO CHILD'S EXPERIENCE

Teacher: Many of you have probably gotten letters in the mail. How can we tell this is a letter?

Child: Someone put their name on it. (*Points to signature.*)

Teacher: Yep, that is exactly how we can tell this is a letter. Mr. Blueberry signed this one.

STAR: Sit Together and Read

Growing Vegetable Soup

TARGET: Page Organization

★ High-Support Examples

1) TECHNIQUE: COPARTICIPATION

Teacher: Let's all point together to the top of the page.

Children: (*Point with the teacher.*)

Teacher: This is the top of the page (*points again*). Now, let's all point to the bottom of the same page.

2) TECHNIQUE: MODELING THE ANSWER

Teacher: I would like to start reading at the very top of this page. Since this is the top of the page, I am going to start reading right here (*points to first words on page and tracks print from left to right*). I'm not going to start here, am I? (*Points to the bottom of the page.*)

Child: No!

Teacher: Right, I need to start up here, at the top.

★ Low-Support Examples

1) TECHNIQUE: ENCOURAGEMENT

Teacher: We've talked about how to find the top of a page and the bottom of a page. Everyone did a wonderful job showing me how to find them. Who can show me the bottom of this page?

Child: I can! (*Points to bottom of the page.*)

Teacher: Wow, you did that quickly, and you are right, this is the bottom of the page.

2) TECHNIQUE: EXPLANATION

Teacher: Let's take a look at this page. Where are the words on this page?

Child: At the top.

Teacher: You're right! The biggest words we see are at the top of the page. I do see words at the bottom, too, but these words are smaller. When we are reading, we need to look at the top of the page and at the bottom of the page for letters and words.

STAR: Sit Together and Read

Growing Vegetable Soup

TARGET: Short Words and Long Words

★ High-Support Examples

1) TECHNIQUE: ELICITING THE ANSWER

Teacher: Let's look at these two words. Just by looking at them, I can tell which word is longer than the other word. The word *the* is a word we see all the time. It is a short word with only three letters in it. The word *package* is a long word. It has seven letters in it. Who can tell me which word is the short word?

Child: *The*!

Teacher: Exactly. The word *the* is much shorter than the word *package*.

2) TECHNIQUE: COPARTICIPATION

Teacher: These three words look shorter than the word *sprouts,* don't they? Let's count the letters in the shorter words (*begins counting with children*). Now let's count the letters in *sprouts* (*begins counting with children*). Seven letters in *sprouts,* and only three letters in each of these words. So, is *sprouts* the long word?

Child: Yes!

Teacher: *Sprouts* is the long word since it has seven letters in it, and the other words we looked at have three letters in them.

★ Low-Support Examples

1) TECHNIQUE: EXPLANATION

Teacher: Without counting the letters in these words, who can tell me which word is the longest?

Child: (*Points to* vegetable.)

Teacher: That's right. *Vegetable* is very long compared to the other words on this page. The words *to* and *or* and *us* we see a lot when we read. They are short words.

2) TECHNIQUE: ENCOURAGEMENT

Teacher: Tammy, you've been working very hard on your reading, so I think you'll be able to point out the shortest word on this page, and the longest word on this page.

Child: (*Points to* sprouts *and* the.)

Teacher: Good job. Now, this is a little tricky—which word is as long as *the*? You found *the*, so I bet you can find it!

STAR: Sit Together and Read

Froggy Gets Dressed

TARGET: Letter Names

★ High-Support Examples

1) TECHNIQUE: ELICITING THE ANSWER

Teacher: Look at all these words that begin with the letter *z*—*zoop, zup, zat, zwit,* and *zum*. There are so many *z*'s on this page! (*Points again to all the z's.*) What is the name of this letter?

Children: (*Call out* z.)

Teacher: Yes, this letter is a *z*. Good job!

2) TECHNIQUE: MODELING THE ANSWER

Teacher: I'll read this page: "And flopped outside into the snow—flop flop flop." I see lots of the same letters! Since I know that this is the letter *f* (*points to first word beginning with* f), I know that this is the letter *f* (*points to next word beginning with* f). They look the same. Who can tell me the name of the first letter in *flop*?

Child: (*Repeats the word* flop.)

Teacher: You said the word *flop* just the right way. That is the whole word. The name of the first letter in *flop is f.*

★ Low-Support Examples

1) TECHNIQUE: RELATING TO THE CHILD'S EXPERIENCE

Teacher: Froggy's mother is calling to him from their house. See where it says *FRRROOGGYY*? Frank, I think you can tell me the name of the first letter in that word, since you use it every day when you write your name!

Child: *F*!

Teacher: I knew you would know the name of that letter. *F* is right!

2) TECHNIQUE: ENCOURAGEMENT

Teacher: We talked earlier about the names of the letters we see in the books we are reading. You all did such a good job at telling me the names of the letters that I pointed to. I'm going to ask you to do that again while we read this book. (*Begins by pointing to the first letters in each of the words in the title.*)

Children: (*Call out the letter names.*)

Teacher: I like how you all are calling out the letter names. You are exactly right. This is *F, G,* and *D*.

STAR: Sit Together and Read

Froggy Gets Dressed

TARGET: Concept of Reading

★ High-Support Examples

1) TECHNIQUE: COPARTICIPATION

Teacher: Let's all put our thinking caps on and list all the things we're going to do when we read Froggy Gets Dressed. I'll start us off. When we read, we're going to read the cover and look at the picture and think about what the book is about. Then we'll turn the pages (*models which way*) and read the words to see if we guessed correctly!

Children: (*Brainstorm on the activity of reading.*)

Teacher: Yes, we are going to turn the pages and look at pictures. And we are going to read to find out what the book is about.

2) TECHNIQUE: MODELING THE ANSWER

Teacher: Who can tell me, just by looking at the cover, what this book is about? I think I know, since I see some snow and a little frog peeking out the window. What do you think our book is about?

Child: It's snowing!

Teacher: I see snow through the window, too. Let's take another look. Who is looking out the window? I think Froggy is looking out the window at the snow, so this book might be about Froggy playing in the snow. Let's see.

★ Low-Support Examples

1) TECHNIQUE: EXPLANATION

Teacher: I think we'll read this book today. The title of the book is Froggy Gets Dressed. What do you think would happen if we started reading right in the middle of the book? Would we really know what the story was about if we started there?

Children: No! You have to start at the beginning!

Teacher: You're right. I need to start at the beginning of the book, which is where the story starts. If I don't do that, then I won't know everything about Froggy, and I won't know how he ended up in the snow without his shirt and coat!

2) TECHNIQUE: PREDICTION

Teacher: How can I find out what happens to Froggy after he goes outside in the snow? Can I put the book down and go outside and play on the swings and still find out what happens to Froggy?

Children: No! You have to read the story.

Teacher: Exactly. If I want to find out what happens, I need to read the pages of this book, every word of it, so that I know why Froggy looks excited about the snow. Swinging on the swings isn't the same thing as reading, not at all!

STAR: Sit Together and Read

I Stink!

TARGET: Concept of Letter

★ High-Support Examples

1) TECHNIQUE: ELICITING THE ANSWER

Teacher: Take a look at the title of this book. It says *I Stink*! And in the title I see the letter *I* here and here. (*Points to both* I*'s in the title.*) Can anyone show me where the letter *I* is in both words?

Child: (*Points to the letters and then to the exclamation point.*)

Teacher: You are right on the first two, but the last one is an exclamation point. That is not a letter. This is the letter *I* and this is the letter *i*.

2) TECHNIQUE: COPARTICIPATION

Teacher: Who can point with me to all the letter *I*'s on this page?

Children: (*Begin pointing with the teacher.*)

Teacher: Excellent! We are pointing to all the letter *I*'s.

★ Low-Support Examples

1) TECHNIQUE: EXPLANATION

Teacher: Who can show me how many times the letter *I* is on this page?

Child: (*Points to the* I*'s in the title.*)

Teacher: Excellent! The letter *I* works to make both the words *I* and *Stink*. It works very hard, like all the letters in the alphabet. I even see one more *I* on the cover. Hmmm, this is tricky. Can anyone else find it? (*Wait to see if children find the* I *in* Scholastic. *Point it out for fun if they don't find it.*)

2) TECHNIQUE: ENCOURAGEMENT

Teacher: I think you all can show me where all of the *I*'s are on this page. Remember we did this before for *Spot Bakes a Cake* and for *Rumble in the Jungle*?

Children: (*Begin pointing to the* I*'s.*)

Teacher: Very nice. Yes, that is an *I*, and so is that. Both are the letter *I*.

STAR: Sit Together and Read

I Stink!

TARGET: Page Order

★ High-Support Examples

1) TECHNIQUE: MODELING THE ANSWER

Teacher: (*Turns to the title page of* I Stink!) I am now looking at this page, the title page. I want to begin reading, so I need to think about which way to turn the page. I think I should turn to this page. Which page do you think I should turn to?

Child: (*Turns back to the cover.*)

Teacher: (*Turns from cover to title page.*) If I am on this page, and I want to start reading, I go this way to the next page to see if that is where the story starts.

2) TECHNIQUE: REDUCING CHOICES/GIVING ALTERNATIVES

Teacher: OK now. I've read this page (*first page of story*), and now I want to keep reading. Which way should I turn the page, this way (*next page of story*) or this way (*back a page*)?

Child: Turn to the next page!

Teacher: Exactly! That is how we read the story.

★ Low-Support Examples

1) TECHNIQUE: PREDICTION

Teacher: I want to go to the last page of our story. Show me which page I need to go to.

Child: (*Turns pages to the last page.*)

Teacher: Yep, if I'm all done reading the story, I am on this page, the last page of our book.

2) TECHNIQUE: ENCOURAGEMENT

Teacher: Philip, I saw you reading your book, and you were turning the pages just the right way. Can you show me how to turn the pages of this book so we can read it together?

Child: (*Begins helping the teacher turn the pages.*)

Teacher: You are doing such a good job. Everyone watch as Philip turns the pages the right way.

STAR: Sit Together and Read

Animal Action ABC

TARGET: Letters and Words

★ High-Support Examples

1) TECHNIQUE: MODELING THE ANSWER

Teacher: We see the letter *E* on this page. *E* is for *elephant*. I'd like to think of more words that start with the letter *E*. I'm going to look around the room to help me find an *E*. *Ethan* (points to child's cubby) starts with *E*. Who else can find an *E*?

Child: And *egg*! Right there. (*Points to the poster.*)

Teacher: You're right! *E* is in the words *egg* and *elephant*. Let's look around some more.

2) TECHNIQUE: ELICITING THE ANSWER

Teacher: *D* is in the word *drink*. Let's find the word *drink* on this page. Here it is. This is the word *drink*. What word is this?

Children: *Drink*!

Teacher: Yes! This is the word *drink*, and *d* is in the word *drink*.

★ Low-Support Examples

1) TECHNIQUE: ENCOURAGEMENT

Teacher: Who knows what this letter is? Marika, I bet you know!

Child: It's the letter *M*. It's in my name!

Teacher: I knew you would get that one. Yes, this is the letter *M*, just like the first letter in Marika's name.

2) TECHNIQUE: PREDICTION

Teacher: What letters do you think we'll see in this book?

Child: *A-B-C*! It's on the front of the book!

Teacher: Let's see! I see lots of different letters in this book. I bet we'll see all different letters!

STAR: Sit Together and Read

Animal Action ABC

TARGET: Letter Names

★ High-Support Examples

1) TECHNIQUE: COPARTICIPATION

Child: It looks like a line! (*Points to the* J.)

Teacher: It does look like a line. That's a *J*. Let's all make a *J* together with our fingers. Watch me!

Children: (*Make the letter* J *in the air.*)

Teacher: Exactly, you all made the letter *J*.

2) TECHNIQUE: MODELING THE ANSWER

Teacher: This is the letter *A* (*points to the* A). And this is the letter *B* (*points to* B). And this is the letter *C* (*points to* C). But now I want to find the letter *A* again. I'll have to go back to the first page to find it. Who can show us the letter *A*?

Child: (*Points to picture of the whale's tail.*)

Teacher: That is a picture of the whale's tail. This is the letter *A*.

★ Low-Support Examples

1) TECHNIQUE: ENCOURAGEMENT

Teacher: What letter does Angel's name start with, can you tell me?

Children: *A*!

Teacher: That's right. Angel's name starts with the letter *A*. Since you know that, I think you can show me where the *A* is on this page.

2) TECHNIQUE: EXPLANATION

Teacher: Let's all stretch our arms out just like this cheetah in the picture. What are we doing with our arms?

Children: Stretching!

Teacher: Listen to the word *stretch*. What letter does *sssssssssstretch* start with?

Children: *S*!

Teacher: Very good. Yes, this is the letter *s* in the word *stretch* on our page. It is the first letter in the word.

STAR: Sit Together and Read

My Backpack

TARGET: Upper- and Lower-Case Forms

★ High-Support Examples

1) TECHNIQUE: ELICITING THE ANSWER

Teacher: Each of these sentences starts with an upper-case letter. (*Points to the first word in each sentence.*) See, this is an upper-case *D* in the word *Dad*. And here we have two uppercase *I*'s in *I* and *I'll*. The last upper-case letter we see is the *H* in *His*. We call these letters *upper-case*. Who can tell me what kind of letters these are?

Child: Big letters!

Teacher: They are bigger than the other letters, and they are at the beginning of each sentence. They are upper-case letters.

2) TECHNIQUE: MODELING THE ANSWER

Teacher: The first letter *M* in *Mom* looks a little different than the last letter *m* in *Mom*, doesn't it? That tells me it must be the upper-case letter. Who can point to the upper-case letter *M* in *Mom*?

Child: (*Points to the lower-case* m.)

Teacher: You've pointed to the lower-case *m*. It's smaller and looks a bit different than this one (*points to the lower-case* m). This is the big upper-case *M*.

★ Low-Support Examples

1) TECHNIQUE: RELATING TO THE CHILD'S EXPERIENCE

Teacher: We've spent some time talking about two different kinds of letters—upper-case and lower-case letters—and we've worked on figuring out which is which. Before we start reading this page, who can point to the upper-case letter *S* on this page?

Child: (*Points correctly to* S *in* She.)

Teacher: That's right. That's an upper-case *S*. Now who can point to the lower-case *m*?

Child: (*Spends time finding all the lower-case* m's *on the page.*)

2) TECHNIQUE: ENCOURAGEMENT

Teacher: Tarieja, you were writing a letter to your dad yesterday and you wrote an upper-case *D* in *Dear* and another upper-case *D* in *Dad*. Can you show me the upper-case *D* on this page? I'm sure you know it.

Child: (*Points correctly to* D.)

Teacher: Excellent, I thought you would remember.

STAR: Sit Together and Read

My Backpack

TARGET: Concept of Words in Print

★ High-Support Examples

1) TECHNIQUE: ELICITING THE ANSWER

Teacher: We're going to read this story called *My Backpack*. Before we do, let's take a look through it. All of these pages have words on them (*selects a page and points to a few words on the page*). Who can point to three different words for me?

Child: (*Points at three words.*)

Teacher: Right! Each of these is a word in the story.

2) TECHNIQUE: REDUCING CHOICES/GIVING ALTERNATIVES

Teacher: I'm looking for a word on this page. Is this a word (*points to a word*) or is this a word (*points to one of the items in the backpack*)?

Child: That's not a word. The boy put that in there!

Teacher: He did put that in his backpack. It's a picture, not a word. This is the word.

★ Low-Support Examples

1) TECHNIQUE: EXPLANATION

Teacher: I see an awful lot of words on this page. And I see one word all by itself. Can anyone point to that word for me?

Child: (*Points to* meow.)

Teacher: You got it! And that was a hard one. The word *meow* is way down here and it's in different colors, but it is still a word!

2) TECHNIQUE: ENCOURAGEMENT

Teacher: Who can find the word on this page? Marcus, I think I see you looking right at it. Can you show me?

Child: (*Points to the picture of the backpack.*)

Teacher: Whoops, not quite. Can you try again? Point to a word on this page.

Child: (*Points to a word.*)

Teacher: There you go! Yes, that is a word!

STAR: Sit Together and Read

Baghead

TARGET: Short Words and Long Words

★ High-Support Examples

1) TECHNIQUE: REDUCE CHOICES/GIVING ALTERNATIVES

   Teacher: Let's see. Which word is longer—*breakfast* or *bag*?

   Child: *Breakfast*!

   Teacher: Exactly. There are only three letters in *bag* and *breakfast* has many more.

2) TECHNIQUE: COPARTICIPATION

   Teacher: Let's look at the words *On* and *Thursday*. *On* is a very short word. It has two letters. *Thursday* looks much longer. And it is! It has eight letters in it. When I point to *On*, call out *short word*! When I point to *Thursday*, call out *long word*! Ready? (*Points to* Thursday.)

   Children: (*Call out both* short word *and* long word.)

   Teacher: I heard some people say *short* and some say *long*. Remember, *On*, with two letters, is a short word, and *Thursday*, right beside it, is the long word with eight letters in it.

★ Low-Support Examples

1) TECHNIQUE: PREDICTION

   Teacher: Who thinks that the word *Thursday* is the longest word on this page? Raise your hands.

   Children: (*Many raise their hands.*)

   Teacher: OK, let's find out by counting the number of letters in each word.

2) TECHNIQUE: EXPLANATION

   Teacher: Let's look at this sentence, "A very big, brown, bag idea." Who can point to the shortest word in this sentence?

   Child: (*Points to* A.)

   Teacher: Good job! *A* is a very, very short word—it only has one letter!

   Teacher: There you go! Yes, that is a word!

STAR: Sit Together and Read

Baghead

TARGET: Print Direction

★ High-Support Examples

1) TECHNIQUE: REDUCE CHOICES/GIVING ALTERNATIVES

Teacher: When we start reading this book, will we read this way (*runs finger right to left over print*) or this way (*runs finger left to right over print*)?

Child: This way (*runs finger left to right*).

Teacher: Yes! It would be silly if we tried to read the other way. We wouldn't know what the story said!

2) TECHNIQUE: ELICITING THE ANSWER

Teacher: When we read a story, we read this way (*sweeps finger left to right*). Which way do we read?

Child: Like this (*runs finger from left to right*).

Teacher: That is exactly right! We read from left to right (*sweeps finger left to right again*).

★ Low-Support Examples

1) TECHNIQUE: ENCOURAGEMENT

Teacher: We have spent a lot of time reading storybooks. I think you all know which way we read the words in storybooks. Put your fingers in the air to show me which way we read.

Children: (*Sweep fingers left to right.*)

Teacher: Yes, you all are so good at this. That is exactly how we read, left to right.

2) TECHNIQUE: EXPLANATION

Teacher: When we read, do we read the words like this (*zigzags finger across the page*)?

Children: No!

Teacher: Right, you knew that. We read each line this way (*runs finger over print left to right*).

STAR: Sit Together and Read

A Color of His Own

TARGET: Page Organization

★ High-Support Examples

1) TECHNIQUE: COPARTICIPATION

Teacher: We've talked before about the top of the page and the bottom of the page (*points to both*). Let's go around the circle. I'll point to the top or the bottom, and when it's your turn, I want you to tell me *top* or *bottom*. Let's start with Jake.

Child: Top!

Teacher: I can't fool you at all. Yes, this is the top of the page.

2) TECHNIQUE: REDUCE CHOICES/GIVING ALTERNATIVES

Teacher: Is this the top of the page (*points to the right side*) or is this the top of the page?

Children: (*Point to the top.*)

Teacher: Wonderful! Yes, this is the top of the page.

★ Low-Support Examples

1) TECHNIQUE: ENCOURAGEMENT

Teacher: Carolyn, you've been doing so much reading. I bet you can tell me which is the top of the page and which is the bottom of the page, can't you? We've talked about this before. Please come up and show me.

Children: This is the top and this is the bottom (*pointing correctly*).

Teacher: Very good. Yes, this is the top and this is the bottom.

2) TECHNIQUE: EXPLANATION

Teacher: Who can show me where the bottom of the page is?

Child: (*Points to bottom.*)

Teacher: You got it! This is the bottom, and this is the top, and we start reading at the top of the page.

STAR: Sit Together and Read

A Color of His Own

TARGET: Concept of Reading

★ High-Support Examples

1) TECHNIQUE: COPARTICIPATION

Teacher: We have read so many stories together this year. Think about the times we've read books together. What are some of the things we do when we read? I'll start. When we read, we pick up the book and look at the title (*points to title*). This will tell us what the book is about. Now someone else tell me what we do when we read.

Child: We look at the pictures.

Teacher: Yes, we do. And we look at the words and figure out where to read.

2) TECHNIQUE: MODELING THE ANSWER

Teacher: The chameleon is green now (*points to chameleon on the green leaf*). Oh, but look here (*points to next page*).The leaf turned yellow and so did the chameleon. It seems like he doesn't have a color of his own at all, just like the book said. I'll need to keep reading to find out what happens to his color. James, what do I need to do to find out what happens to the little chameleon's color?

Child: Keep looking at the book!

Teacher: Exactly. We'll keep reading the book to find out more about the chameleon's color.

★ Low-Support Examples

1) TECHNIQUE: PREDICTION

Teacher: How many of you think this book is about a duck?

Children: (*Some raise hands.*)

Teacher: How many of you think this book is about an animal called a chameleon?

Children: (*Some raise hands.*)

Teacher: Hmmm, we're not sure. How will we find out?

Children: Read the story!

Teacher: Yes! We must read the story to see if it is about a duck or a chameleon.

2) TECHNIQUE: ENCOURAGEMENT

Teacher: After reading all these storybooks together, I'll bet we can go around the room and you can each tell me something we do, or something we learn, from reading. Cameron, you start.

Child: A chameleon changes colors.

Teacher: We did learn that chameleons change colors. That is right!

STAR: Sit Together and Read

To Market, to Market

TARGET: Word Identification

★ High-Support Examples

1) TECHNIQUE: ELICITING THE ANSWER

Teacher: This word says *pig*. Who can tell me what this word is?

Child: *Pig*!

Teacher: You are exactly right. This pink word says *pig*.

2) TECHNIQUE: MODELING THE ANSWER

Teacher: I'm looking for the word *cow* on this page. Where can I find *cow*? I'll start reading and tell you when I come to it. (*Reads sentence aloud*.) Ah! Here it is, this word says *cow*! Who knows this word?

Child: *Cow*!

Teacher: This word is *cow*. You all knew that.

★ Low-Support Examples

1) TECHNIQUE: EXPLANATION

Teacher: Who knows what this word is? (*point to* market)?

Child: *Market*!

Teacher: Excellent! Yes, this word says *market*. You knew that since we read it in the title, and we knew that she was going to buy food at the market.

2) TECHNIQUE: PREDICTION

Teacher: This book is called *To Market, to Market*. Hmmm, who can tell me what words we might find in this book if it is about going to the grocery store? Give me some words, and then we'll see if we can find them as we read.

Child: *Pig, milk, cereal*!

Teacher: Those are great guesses. Let's keep reading and see.

STAR: Sit Together and Read

To Market, to Market

TARGET: Print Direction

★ High-Support Examples

1) TECHNIQUE: REDUCING CHOICES/GIVING ALTERNATIVES

Teacher: Should I start to read here (*points to* zoo), or should I start to read here (*points to* The)?

Child: Start up there. (*Points to* The.)

Teacher: Exactly right, that is right where I'll start reading.

2) TECHNIQUE: ELICITING THE ANSWER

Teacher: When we read, we start on the left side (*points to left side*) and we go this way (*gesturing with finger across sentence*). Who can point to where we start reading on this page? Come on up, Michael, and show us.

Child: (*Points to the left side of page.*)

Teacher: Yes. Good. We start right here (*pointing again to left side of page*).

★ Low-Support Examples

1) TECHNIQUE: ENCOURAGEMENT

Teacher: We've talked a lot lately about the way we read the words on the page of a book. I think you can show me which way to read. Which way do I read, this way or this way (*running finger over sentence from left to right and then from right to left*)? Remember, we talked about this yesterday.

Child: I know! This way (*running finger through air from left to right*).

Teacher: You got it. You remembered! We read from left to right.

2) TECHNIQUE: PREDICTION

Teacher: If I started reading here and went this way (*points to end of sentence and tracks right to left*), would I know what this sentence said?

Child: No! You can't read that way, the words have to go this way. (*Points left to right.*)

Teacher: I better read your way so I know what the page says. (*Sweeps finger left to right.*)

STAR: Sit Together and Read

Hey, Little Ant

TARGET: Title of Book

★ High-Support Examples

1) TECHNIQUE: ELICITING THE ANSWER

Teacher: This is the title of the book. It tells us the name of the book. Who can tell me what a title does?

Child: It tells the name of the book!

Teacher: Yes, and the title of this book is *Hey, Little Ant.*

2) TECHNIQUE: COPARTICIPATION

Teacher: Cameron, please come up here and point to the title of this book with me. I'll help.

Child: (*Joins teacher at the book.*)

Teacher: Put your finger on mine, and we'll point to the title. Just like that. Very good!

★ Low-Support Examples

1) TECHNIQUE: PREDICTION

Teacher: Where do you think we can find the title of the book?

Child: On the front of the book and on the next page.

Teacher: Absolutely, the title is on the front of the book, and then we can see it on the title page. I'm so proud you remembered the title page!

2) TECHNIQUE: RELATING TO THE CHILD'S EXPERIENCE

Teacher: Julio, you told us that you have this book at home and that you've read it before. Can you tell us what the title is again?

Child: *Little Ant*!

Teacher: Very good. There is one more word in the title. Take another look. What is the whole title of the book?

Child: *Hey, Little Ant*!

STAR: Sit Together and Read

Hey, Little Ant

TARGET: Upper- and Lower-Case Forms

★ High-Support Examples

1) TECHNIQUE: ELICITING THE ANSWER

Teacher: I see three upper-case letters (*pointing to the title*). There is an upper-case *H*, an upper-case *L*, and an upper-case *A* (*pointing to each letter in turn*). Khara, will you come up here and point to one of the upper-case letters?

Child: (*Points to the letter* H.)

Teacher: Excellent! Thank you. Can you point to the other two upper-case letters?

2) TECHNIQUE: REDUCE CHOICES/GIVING ALTERNATIVES

Teacher: Is this an upper-case letter (*points to the* H) or is this an upper-case letter (*points to the* t)?

Children: (*Call out that the* H *is the upper-case letter.*)

Teacher: Very good. You are right, the H is the upper-case letter, the *t* is a lower-case letter.

★ Low-Support Examples

1) TECHNIQUE: EXPLANATION

Teacher: Is this an upper-case letter or a lower-case letter? (*Points to the* A *in* Anyone*)*?

Children: (*Call out that it is an upper-case letter.*)

Teacher: Exactly. And we know that this *A* is an upper-case letter because of the way it looks, and because it is the start of this sentence.

2) TECHNIQUE: RELATING TO THE CHILD'S EXPERIENCE

Teacher: Brian, come on up here and point to the upper-case *B* in this sentence. That upper-case *B* will look familiar to you!

Child: It's in my name. It's right here. (*Points correctly.*)

Teacher: There you go. *B* as in *Brian*!

STAR: Sit Together and Read

Mouse Mess

TARGET: Environmental Print

★ High-Support Examples

1) TECHNIQUE: MODELING THE ANSWER

Teacher: We see lots of words on this page, like here and here. Let's look carefully to see if we can find other words. Remember, we have to look for words and letters. They might be in funny, surprising places, like on this jar that says *Peanut Butter*. Can you show me another place on this page where we see words?

Child: Here!

Teacher: Yes, we see words on the cereal box and on the jar of jam! Surprise! Under the word *jam* it says *Raspberry*.

2) TECHNIQUE: COPARTICIPATION

Teacher: Let's find all the letters and words on this can. Here is a word, and here are the letters. Now you show me like I showed you.

Child: OK, here and here. (*Points to* sardines *and the letters.*)

Teacher: Wonderful. You are right. Here is a word, and here is a letter. The word says *sardines*, and this is the letter *s* in *sardines*.

★ Low-Support Examples

1) TECHNIQUE: RELATING TO THE CHILD'S EXPERIENCE

Teacher: Take a look at this box and the bowl. Does it look familiar? What kind of cereal do you eat?

Child: Corn flakes!

Teacher: Me, too! What do you think the box says?

Child: *Corn flakes*!

Teacher: Yes, corn flakes. See, *corn ... flakes*. (*Points to each word.*)

2) TECHNIQUE: EXPLANATION

Teacher: Can you point to a word on this page?

Child: Here!

Teacher: That's right! The words on this jar say *Peanut Butter*. That tells us that this is the peanut butter jar!

STAR: Sit Together and Read

Mouse Mess

TARGET: Page Order

★ High-Support Examples

1) TECHNIQUE: ELICITING THE ANSWER

Teacher: This is the way I turn the page. Which way do I turn the page?

Child: This way!

Teacher: That is exactly right. I turn the page this way.

2) TECHNIQUE: REDUCE CHOICES/GIVING ALTERNATIVES

Teacher: Do I turn the page this way (*turns the pages right to left*) or this way (*turns the pages left to right*)?

Child: This way? (*Turns the page left to right.*)

Teacher: Almost, this is the way I turn the page.

★ Low-Support Examples

1) TECHNIQUE: ENCOURAGEMENT

Teacher: Where do you think the top of the page is? Spencer, I know you'll know this because you knew it before!

Child: Right here?

Teacher: That's right! This is the top, just like you said before.

2) TECHNIQUE: EXPLANATION

Teacher: Can you show me the top of the page?

Child: Here?

Teacher: That's right! The top of the page is right here, and that's where we find the words to start reading!

STAR: Sit Together and Read

In the Small, Small Pond

TARGET: Concept of Word in Print

★ High-Support Examples

1) TECHNIQUE: COPARTICIPATION

Teacher: Shannon, come on up here and point to all the words on this page with me.

Child: (*Points to the picture of the frog.*)

Teacher: That is a picture of the frog we'll be chasing in the book. Here, I'll point to each word, and you point to each after me.

2) TECHNIQUE: MODELING THE ANSWER

Teacher: I know that there are two words on this page. I'm going to count the words on this page to make sure I find each one. I have to look for words, not pictures. Now, Demetrius, you come up and count all the words on this page.

Child: Here's a word.

Teacher: Nice job! You found a word that I did, too. What other word did I find?

★ Low-Support Examples

1) TECHNIQUE: ENCOURAGEMENT

Teacher: We have been talking about words for a long time now. I bet you all can tell me how many words are on this page. Look carefully!

Children: (*Call out the number of words.*)

Teacher: Very good! I heard everyone call out *two*, and that is correct!

2) TECHNIQUE: EXPLANATION

Teacher: Who can tell me how many words are on this page?

Child: Two!

Teacher: Yep, two words on this page. We know this since we see the words here (*points to words*), and the rest of the page has a picture of fish on it.

STAR: Sit Together and Read

In the Small, Small Pond

TARGET: Print Direction

★ High-Support Examples

1) TECHNIQUE: COPARTICIPATION

Teacher: OK, let's get ready to read this page. Cameron, please come up here with me and let's point to where we'll start reading.

Child: (*Points to the picture of the heron.*)

Teacher: We don't start there since there aren't any words. Let's get help looking for the word we'll read first. Dominique, come help us.

Child: (*Looks at book with teacher.*)

Teacher: Here we go. This is where we start. Each of you point to the first word.

2) TECHNIQUE: REDUCE CHOICES/GIVING ALTERNATIVES

Teacher: This is the beginning of our story. Do I start reading here (*points to* pond *the last word on the page*), or do I start here (*points to* In *the first word on the page*)?

Child: To the word!

Teacher: Exactly. I have to start with *In* since that is the first word on this page. And we start reading on this page.

★ Low-Support Examples

1) TECHNIQUE: RELATING TO THE CHILD'S EXPERIENCE

Teacher: Tamara, you've looked at a lot of books lately. I'll bet you can show us where we should start reading. Will you come up and point to the place we start reading?

Child: (*Points to the first word.*)

Teacher: I do start there. It didn't fool you that the first word is in the middle of the page!

2) TECHNIQUE: EXPLANATION

Teacher: Where will I start reading on this page? This is a tricky one! Lakeesha, can you tell us where I'll start reading? Come up and show us.

Child: Right here (*points to* wiggle)?

Teacher: Exactly right. This wasn't tricky for you. We start with *wiggle* because it is all the way over here, to the left. This word, *jiggle,* starts further over. And we know we read left to right.

STAR: Sit Together and Read

The Grumpy Morning

TARGET: Letter Names

★ High-Support Examples

1) TECHNIQUE: MODELING THE ANSWER

Teacher: Look at this funny page. All the animals are talking. I see lots of letters on this page since the animals are talking so much. Here is an *M* and here is an *O*. Tracey, come on up here and show us where you find the *M*. I just want to find a couple of letters, and since there is a cow in the picture, I bet I can find *M* and *O* for *MOOO*.

Child: (*Points to the* M.) Here.

Teacher: Wonderful. Now will you point to the letter *O*?

2) TECHNIQUE: REDUCING CHOICES/GIVING ALTERNATIVES

Teacher: Is this the letter *S* (points to the *I*) or is this the letter *S* (points to the *S*)?

Child: The squiggly one!

Teacher: The letter *S* is squiggly, isn't it? You are right. This is the letter *S*.

★ Low-Support Examples

1) TECHNIQUE: PREDICTION

Teacher: What is this a picture of, does anyone know?

Children: It's a goat!

Teacher: Yes, you're right. Can anyone guess what letter we might find on this page if it has a picture of a goat on it? I'll give you a hint—what letter does *goat* start with?

Children: *G*!

Teacher: I think you are right. Let's look for the *G*.

2) TECHNIQUE: ENCOURAGEMENT

Teacher: I see lots of *M*'s on this page. Megan, I bet you know where this letter is since you use it to spell your name. Come show us.

Child: I know *M*. Right here, and here is another one.

Teacher: Oh, my goodness. You found another one. I see one more, do you?

STAR: Sit Together and Read

The Grumpy Morning

TARGET: Concept of Reading

★ High-Support Examples

1) TECHNIQUE: ELICITING THE ANSWER

Teacher: The title of this book is *The Grumpy Morning*. Look at the animals on the cover. I think we might read about animals and what they do in the morning. Who can tell me what we might read about in this book?

Child: The duck.

Teacher: I see the duck, yes. I bet he is in the story. And I bet we'll find out what he and the other animals do in the morning.

2) TECHNIQUE: REDUCING CHOICES/GIVING ALTERNATIVES

Teacher: This book is called *The Grumpy Morning*, and there are animals on the front cover. Do you think we'll read about how to build a bicycle, or will we read about animals when they get up in the morning?

Child: Animals!

Teacher: Animals is right. This book is about animals in the morning.

★ Low-Support Examples

1) TECHNIQUE: PREDICTION

Teacher: Let's look at the cover of this book. The title is *The Grumpy Morning*. Who can tell me what we might read about in this book?

Child: We'll read about the morning.

Teacher: You are right. What do you think we'll find out about the morning?

2) TECHNIQUE: RELATING TO THE CHILD'S EXPERIENCE

Teacher: We are going to read this book called *The Grumpy Morning*. When we read, what kinds of things do we do? Carrie, I saw you reading a book this morning. What were some of the things you did while you read the book?

Child: I sat down and looked at the book.

Teacher: And what else did you do? Did you look for anything on the pages?

Child: I found words and pictures in the book!

Teacher: I'm sure you did! Can anyone else tell me what they do when they read?

STAR: Sit Together and Read

The Noisy Airplane Ride

TARGET: Letters and Words

★ High-Support Examples

1) TECHNIQUE: ELICITING THE ANSWER

    Teacher: This book is called *The Noisy Airplane Ride*. Look at all the letters in the word *Airplane* (spells out the word letter by letter). I see an *A* in the word *Airplane* (*points to the letter* A). This is the letter *A*. Can someone show us the *A*?

    Child: (*Points to the letter.*)

    Teacher: Right, that is the letter *A*.

2) TECHNIQUE: MODELING THE ANSWER

    Teacher: I'm going to look for a word on this page. Hmmm, this is a word, and this is a word (*points to* Thumpity *and* Thump), but this is not a word (*points to the* p *in* Thump). That is the letter *p* which helps make the word *Thump*. Tyana, will you come up here and point to one of the words on this page?

    Child: (*Points to* Thump.)

    Teacher: That is the word *Thump*. Don't forget that this is a word, too, *Thumpity*.

★ Low-Support Examples

1) TECHNIQUE: ENCOURAGEMENT

    Teacher: This is the word *roar*. Tori, you showed us the letters that make up the word *roar* yesterday. Come up and show us again.

    Child: (*Points to each letter.*)

    Teacher: Good work, just like yesterday. Those are the letters in *roar*.

2) TECHNIQUE: EXPLANATION

    Teacher: Is this a word, or is this a letter (*points to the word* Ding)?

    Children: (*Call out* word!)

    Teacher: Exactly. This is a word. This (*points to the letter* D) is a letter, and this letter helps make the word *Ding*.

STAR: Sit Together and Read

The Noisy Airplane Ride

TARGET: Function of Print

★ High-Support Examples

1) TECHNIQUE: COPARTICIPATION

Teacher: OK, these words say *Thrum, Thrum, Thrum!* They tell us what the airplane sounds like when it is in the air. Say the words with me while I point to each one.

Children: (Call out *Thrum, Thrum, Thrum!*)

Teacher: Thank you for saying *Thrum* each time I pointed. Good work!

2) TECHNIQUE: ELICITING THE ANSWER

Teacher: This word says *Clunk. Clunk* is the sound the wheels make when they go up into the belly of the airplane. We can use words to make noises. What can we use words for?

Children: Noises!

Teacher: That's right. *Pop* is another word that is a noise.

★ Low-Support Examples

1) TECHNIQUE: PREDICTION

Teacher: This book is called *The Noisy Airplane Ride*. It's about a boy taking a ride in an airplane and all the sounds he'll hear. What are some words you think we'll find in this book?

Children: All the sounds in the plane.

Teacher: Good. What word do you think we'll see when the plane goes very, very fast on the ground?

Children: *Whoosh!*

Teacher: That is a wonderful word! I hope we see it. The word might look long and thin and all stretched out, like it is racing on the page.

2) TECHNIQUE: ENCOURAGEMENT

Teacher: Take a look at this page with all these words on it. I know you all can tell me what these words are saying, since we talked about the kinds of sounds we hear when people are walking up and down the hall.

Children: (*Call out various words they remember.*)

Teacher: *Thud* is one, yes! And so is *stomp*. Let's all stomp our feet. Ready, set, stomp!

STAR: Sit Together and Read

How to Speak Moo!

TARGET: Title of Book

★ High-Support Examples

1) TECHNIQUE: ELICITING THE ANSWER

Teacher: The title of this book is *How to Speak Moo!* It tells us the name of the book. Who can tell me what the title does?

Child: Tells us the name of the book.

Teacher: Wonderful! The title tells us the name of the book.

2) TECHNIQUE: MODELING THE ANSWER

Teacher: I'm going to look for the title of this book. And I know I'm going to find it on the front where I usually do. Here it is, *How to Speak Moo!* Who can tell me where I can find the title of a book?

Children: On the front!

Teacher: On the front! Yes.

★ Low-Support Examples

1) TECHNIQUE: ENCOURAGEMENT

Teacher: We've talked a lot about the titles of books and what they do. Tell me again what the title does for us?

Children: Tells us what we're going to read about.

Teacher: Perfect! That is an important job for the title—to tell us what the book is about.

2) TECHNIQUE: EXPLANATION

Teacher: Marcus, can you tell us what the title does?

Child: It tells us what we're going to read.

Teacher: Exactly. The title is on the front of the book, so we know what the book will be about.

STAR: Sit Together and Read

How to Speak Moo!

TARGET: Word Identification

★ High-Support Examples

1) TECHNIQUE: COPARTICIPATION

Teacher: This word says *Moo* (*points to word in title*). Say *Moo* with me, just like a cow would!

Teacher and Children: (*Call out* moo.)

Teacher: We all sound like a cow. *Moo!*

2) TECHNIQUE: ELICITING THE ANSWER

Teacher: This word is *soft*. That means that the cow's moo will be very quiet, like when we use our library voices. What does this word say? Whisper!

Children: Soft!

Teacher: I'm so happy you used your soft library voices. This word is *soft*.

★ Low-Support Examples

1) TECHNIQUE: PREDICTION

Teacher: Look at the cover of this book. It looks like it's going to be about some cows. What word do you think we might find in this book?

Children: *Cow! Moo!*

Teacher: I bet we find both of those words in this story. Who can point to the word *Moo* in the title?

2) TECHNIQUE: RELATING TO THE CHILD'S EXPERIENCE

Teacher: Walter, this is your favorite book, and I know you've read it before. Can you point to the word *cow* on this page for us?

Children: This is *cow*. This is the picture of the cow.

Teacher: Wow! You showed us the word *cow* and then made sure we saw the picture. Thank you!

STAR: Sit Together and Read

Kindergarten Rocks

TARGET: Author of Book

★ High-Support Examples

1) TECHNIQUE: ELICITING THE ANSWER

Teacher: The author of the book *Kindergarten Rocks* is Katie Davis. She wrote the book we're going to read. Can anyone tell me what the author does?

Child: Wrote the book!

Teacher: Yep, and now we'll read it!

2) TECHNIQUE: REDUCING CHOICES/GIVING ALTERNATIVES

Teacher: The author of this book is Katie Davis. Does an author drive a fire truck, or does an author write books?

Children: Write books!

Teacher: An author writes books. Let's see what Miss Davis wrote about.

★ Low-Support Examples

1) TECHNIQUE: ENCOURAGEMENT

Teacher: Tom, you asked me the author's name, and we talked about it. Do you remember what an author does?

Child: She writes the story.

Teacher: That's right! Katie Davis is the author who wrote the story.

2) TECHNIQUE: EXPLANATION

Teacher: Who can tell me what the author does?

Child: Writes the book!

Teacher: Yep, an author writes the book. And this time the author of our book also drew all the pictures. It says so right here (*points to the cover and reads* Written and Illustrated by Katie Davis). She was very busy because she was the author and the illustrator!

STAR: Sit Together and Read

Kindergarten Rocks

TARGET: Environmental Print

★ High-Support Examples

1) TECHNIQUE: MODELING THE ANSWER

Teacher: Wow, I see words in bubbles on this page. Look, here and here (*points to the bubbles*). Dexter's sister is saying "It's next week, Dexter!" Now how do I know that Dexter's sister is talking? I can tell she is talking because the words are right here, real close to her head. Ricardo, can you come up and point to the words that Dexter's sister is saying?

Child: (*Points to the words in the speech bubble.*)

Teacher: Wonderful! You pointed right to the words that Dexter is saying.

2) TECHNIQUE: COPARTICIPATION

Teacher: Andrea, come up here with me and let's point to all the places on this page where we see words. There sure are a lot of them.

Child: (*Begins pointing with the teacher to* September, Sunday).

Teacher: You are doing good work with me, pointing to all these words that we find in the pictures.

★ Low-Support Examples

1) TECHNIQUE: EXPLANATION

Teacher: Lucy, will you show me where one of the children is talking on this page?

Child: (*Points to* Oh no).

Teacher: That's right. Dexter says "Oh no" because he spills his milk. Is that something you all would say if that happened to you?

2) TECHNIQUE: RELATING TO THE CHILD'S EXPERIENCE

Teacher: I see words on this page. Mary, do you see words on this page? I bet you recognize them since we see these words at our school all the time, especially in the library.

Child: I see the words on the posters.

Teacher: Exactly. This is the library, so what do you think this word is (*pointing to* books)?

Child: Book?

Teacher: Right again! It's *books*. Our library has many posters with the word *book* on them.

STAR: Sit Together and Read

The Recess Queen

TARGET: Short Words and Long Words

★ High-Support Examples

1) TECHNIQUE: ELICITING THE ANSWER

Teacher: Let's take a look at the words on this page. This word *scared* is much longer than this word *if*, isn't it? Who can tell me which word is longer, *scared* or *if*?

Child: *If*!

Teacher: Let's see. *If* has two letters and *scared* has six letters. Since six is more than two, the longest word is *scared*.

2) TECHNIQUE: REDUCING CHOICES/GIVING ALTERNATIVES

Teacher: Which word is longer, *popcorn* or *tea* (*points to each word*)?

Children: *Popcorn*!

Teacher: You got it! *Popcorn* is definitely longer than *tea*. But let's make sure and count the letters.

★ Low-Support Examples

1) TECHNIQUE: EXPLANATION

Teacher: Who can point to a very long word on this page?

Child: (*Points to* lollalooshed.)

Teacher: Yes! That is a very long word. It looks long compared to the rest of the words, and it has 14 letters in it (*pointing and counting to each letter*)!

2) TECHNIQUE: ENCOURAGEMENT

Teacher: The title of this book is *The Recess Queen*. We've been talking about words and how some words are long and some words are short. Annie, can you point to the really short word in the title?

Child: This is the word *The*.

Teacher: And it only has three letters, so you are exactly right. Thank you.

STAR: Sit Together and Read

The Recess Queen

TARGET: Author of Book

★ High-Support Examples

1) TECHNIQUE: COPARTICIPATION

Teacher: We know that the author is the person who writes the book that we are going to read. Tell me again, all together with me, what the author does!

Teacher and Children: Writes the book!

2) TECHNIQUE: ELICITING THE ANSWER

Teacher: Our book today is called *The Recess Queen*. Our author's name is Alexis O'Neill (*points to the name*). That means she wrote the book. What does an author do again?

Children: Writes the book!

Teacher: Yes, the author writes the book.

★ Low-Support Examples

1) TECHNIQUE: EXPLANATION

Teacher: James, come up and point to the name of the author of our book.

Child: (*Points to both names.*)

Teacher: Exactly, those are the people who worked on this book. But, one of them wrote it, while the other one drew the pictures. Let's find out by looking at the back. This is a tricky one! (*Turns to back of book jacket.*) Here it tells us about Alexis O'Neill and that she wrote the book. Here it tells us how Laura Huliska-Beith drew the pictures. So Alexis O'Neill is the author and Laura Huliska-Beith is the illustrator. That was confusing, but now we know!

2) TECHNIQUE: ENCOURAGEMENT

Teacher: Michele, tell us what the author of a book does? You got this right last time!

Children: The author writes the words!

Teacher: The author writes the words, writes the book. Right!

STAR: Sit Together and Read

Miss Bindergarten Gets Ready for Kindergarten

TARGET: Concept of Word in Print

★ High-Support Examples

1) TECHNIQUE: REDUCING CHOICES/GIVING ALTERNATIVES

Teacher: Is this a word (*points to the picture of the blocks in the basket*) or is this a word (*points to the word* kindergarten)?

Child: These are words (*points to* for *and* kindergarten).

Teacher: Yes, you're right. Those are the words on the page. These are the pictures.

2) TECHNIQUE: COPARTICIPATION

Teacher: Anita, come up and point to all the words on this page with me. We have to look carefully since there are words where we might not expect them to be!

Teacher and Child: (*Point together to the words.*)

Teacher: Wonderful job! And this word is *Ready.*

★ Low-Support Examples

1) TECHNIQUE: RELATING TO THE CHILD'S EXPERIENCE

Teacher: There are lots of words on this page, not just at the bottom. Chris, come up and let's see if we can find them. I think you will, since we have our names on the cubbies in this classroom.

Child: Are these names (*pointing to bins*)?

Teacher: Good job! You found the bins with names on them. Those are like our cubbies with names on them.

2) TECHNIQUE: EXPLANATION

Teacher: Addie, come up and point to the words you can find on this page.

Child: (*Points to the words at the bottom and those found within the picture.*)

Teacher: Excellent. Here we have just letters (*points to alphabet strip*), and here we have lots of words (*points to the bins*).

STAR: Sit Together and Read

Miss Bindergarten Gets Ready for Kindergarten

TARGET: Letters and Words

★ High-Support Examples

1) TECHNIQUE: MODELING THE ANSWER

Teacher: Look at this word *bunny*. It has five letters in it, *b-u-n-n-y—bunny* (*points to all the letters while counting*). The letters are all making up this word *bunny*. Who can tell me what this word is?

Children: *Bunny*!

Teacher: And how many letters are in *bunny*?

Children: Five!

Teacher: Good job! This is one word *bunny* with five letters in it.

2) TECHNIQUE: REDUCING CHOICES/GIVING ALTERNATIVES

Teacher: Is this a word (*points to* Kindergarten) or is this a word (*points to the* K *in* Kindergarten)?

Children: No, that's the word (*when the teacher points back to* Kindergarten).

Teacher: Of course, you are right! This is the word *Kindergarten* and this is the letter *K*.

★ Low-Support Examples

1) TECHNIQUE: RELATING TO THE CHILD'S EXPERIENCE

Teacher: Henry, come on up here and let's take a look at this page and see if we can find the letter H and the word that it helps to make. I think you'll find it pretty quickly, since you know this word very well!

Child: It's my name!

Teacher: You get it! Your name is Henry, and it is written right here. And this is the letter *H* that starts your name.

2) TECHNIQUE: EXPLANATION

Teacher: Tracey, please help us find the word *go* on this page.

Child: (Points to *go*).

Teacher: Exactly right. This is the word *go*, and it is made up of two letters, *g-o*.

STAR: Sit Together and Read

References

Adams, M. J. (2002). Alphabetic anxiety and explicit, systematic phonics instruction: A cognitive science perspective. In S. B. Neuman & D. K. Dickinson (Eds.), *Handbook of early literacy research* (Vol. 1, pp. 66–80). New York: Guilford Press.

Adams, M. J., Foorman, B. R., Lundberg, I., & Beeler, T. (1998). *Phonemic awareness in young children: A classroom curriculum.* Baltimore: Brookes.

Alborough, J. (2009). *Hug.* Cambridge, MA: Candlewick.

Andreae, D., & Wojtowycz, D. (1996). *Rumble in the jungle.* London: Little Tiger Press.

Anthony, J. (1997). *The dandelion seed.* Nevada City, CA: Dawn.

Anthony, J. L., Lonigan, C. J., Driscoll, K., Phillips, B. M., & Burgess, S. R. (2003). Phonological sensitivity: A quasi-parallel progression of word structure units and cognitive operations. *Reading Research Quarterly, 38*(4), 470–487.

Aram, D., & Biron, S. (2004). Joint storybook reading and joint writing interventions among low SES preschoolers: Differential contributions to early literacy. *Early Childhood Research Quarterly, 19,* 588–610.

Bear, D. R., Invernizzi, M., Templeton, S., & Johnston, F. (2000). *Words their way: Phonics, spelling, and vocabulary instruction, K–8* (2nd ed.). Columbus, OH: Merrill/Prentice Hall.

Beck, I. L., McKeown, M. G., & Kucan, L. (2002). *Bringing words to life: Robust vocabulary instruction.* New York: Guilford Press.

Biemiller, A., & Boote, C. (2006). An effective method for building meaning vocabulary in primary grades. *Journal of Educational Psychology, 98*(1), 44–62.

Blanc, G. (1990). Vygotsky: The man and his cause. In L. C. Moll (Ed.), *Vygotsky and education: Instructional implications and applications of sociohistorical psychology* (pp. 31–58). New York: Cambridge University Press.

Brett, J. (1989). *The mitten.* New York: Scholastic.

Bridwell, N. (2002). *Clifford goes to dog school.* New York: Scholastic.

Bunting, E. (2005). *My backpack.* Honesdale, PA: Boyds Mills Press.

Cain, J. (2000). *The way I feel.* Seattle: Parenting Press.

Catts, H. W., Fey, M. E., Tomblin, J. B., & Zhang, X. (2002). A longitudinal investigation of reading outcomes in children with language impairment. *Journal of Speech, Language, and Hearing Research, 45,* 1142–1157.

Cazet, D. (1990). *Never spit on your shoes.* New York: Orchard Books.

Cleary, B. P. (2006). *A lime, a mime, and a pool of slime.* Minneapolis: Millbrook Press.

Cronin, D. (2002). *Giggle, giggle, quack.* New York: Scholastic.

Curtis, J. L. & Cornell, L. (2002). *I'm gonna like me.* New York: Joanna Cotler Books.

Curtis, J. L. (2000). *Where do balloons go?* New York: Joanna Cotler Books.

Curtis, J. L., & Cornell, L. (2008). *Big words for little people.* New York: Joanna Cotler Books.

Cuyler, M. (2008). *Monster mess.* New York: Margaret K. McElderry Books.

Daly, C. (2008). *One ridonculous adventure.* New York: Disney Press.

Davis, K. (2005). *Kindergarten rocks!* New York: Harcourt.

Dewdney, A. (2005). *Llama llama red pajama.* New York: Penguin.

Dewdney, A. (2007). *Llama llama mad at mama.* New York: Penguin.

Diaz, R. M., Neal, C., & Vachio, A. (1991). Maternal teaching in the zone of proximal development: A comparison of low- and high-risk dyads. *Merrill–Palmer Quarterly, 37*(1), 83–107.

Downs, M. (2005). *The noisy airplane ride.* Berkeley, CA: Tricycle Press.

Edwards, P. D. (1998). *The grumpy morning.* New York: Scholastic.

Ehlert, L. (1987). *Growing vegetable soup.* San Diego: Harcourt.

Ehlert, L. (1991). *Red leaf, yellow leaf.* New York: Scholastic.

Ernst, L. C. (1996). *The letters are lost.* New York: Scholastic.

Evans, M. A., & Saint-Aubin, J. (2005). What children are looking at during shared storybook reading: Evidence from eye movements. *Psychological Science, 16,* 913–920.

Evans, M. A., Williamson, K., & Pursoo, T. (2008). Preschoolers' attention to print during shared book reading. *Scientific Studies of Reading, 12,* 106–129.

Ezell, H. K., & Justice, L. M. (2000). Increasing the print focus of shared reading interactions through observational learning. *American Journal of Speech–Language Pathology, 9,* 36–47.

Ezell, H. K., Justice, L. M., & Parsons, D. (2000). A clinic-based book reading intervention for parents and their preschoolers with communication impairment. *Child Language Teaching and Therapy, 16,* 121–140.

Fajerman, D. (2002). *How to speak moo!* Hauppauge, NY: Barron's.

Fey, M. E. (1986). *Language intervention with young children.* Austin, TX: PRO-ED.

Figueroa, A. (2004). *Clifford for president.* New York: Scholastic.

Fleming, D. (1993). *In the small, small pond.* New York: Henry & Holt.

Foorman, B. R., Fletcher, J. M., Francis, D. J., Schatschneider, C., & Mehta, P. (1998). The role of instruction in learning to read: Preventing reading failure in at-risk children. *Journal of Educational Psychology, 90*(1), 37–55.

Greene, R. G. (2001). *Jamboree day.* New York: Scholastic.

Halliday, M. A. K. (1975). *Learning how to mean: Explorations in the development of language.* London: Edward Arnold.

Hallinan, P. K. (1987). *My first day of school.* Nashville, TN: Ideals Children's Books.

Hammett, L. A., van Kleeck, A., & Huberty, C. J. (2003). Patterns of parents' extratextual interactions during book sharing with preschool children: A cluster analysis study. *Reading Research Quarterly, 38,* 442–468.

Hammill, D. D. (2004). What we know about correlates of reading. *Exceptional Children, 70,* 453–468.

Hill, E. (1994). *Spot bakes a cake.* New York: Puffin Books.

Hodson, B. (1989). Phonological remediation: A cycles approach. In N. Creaghead, P. Newman, & W. Secord (Eds.), *Assessment and remediation of articulatory and phonological disorders.* Columbus, OH: Merrill.

Hoose, P. M., & Hoose, H. (1998). *Hey, little ant!* Berkeley, CA: Tricycle Press.

Hunter, A. (1998). *Possum and the peeper.* New York: Houghton Mifflin.

Hunter, J. N. (2006). *When daddy's truck picks me up.* Morton Grove: Albert Whitman.

James, S. (1996). *Dear Mr. Blueberry.* New York: Aladdin.

Jenkins, E. (2008). *The little bit scary people.* New York: Hyperion Books for Children.

Jenkins, M. (1999). *The emperor's egg.* Cambridge: Candlewick Press.

Jenkins, S. & Page, R. (2006). *Move.* Boston: Houghton Mifflin.

Jenkins, S. (2004). *Actual size.* Boston: Houghton Mifflin.

Jennings, C. S. (2007). *Animal band.* New York: Sterling.

Joosse, B. (2008). *In the night garden.* New York: Henry Holt.

Justice, L. M., Bowles, R. P., & Skibbe, L. E. (2006). Measuring preschool attainment of print concept knowledge: A study of typical and at-risk 3- to 5-year-old children using item response theory. *Language, Speech and Hearing Services in Schools, 37,* 224–235.

Justice, L. M., Chow, S. M., Capellini, C., Flanigan, K., & Colton, S. (2003). Emergent literacy intervention for vulnerable preschoolers: Relative effects of two approaches. *American Journal of Speech–Language Pathology, 12,* 320–332.

Justice, L. M., & Ezell, H. K. (1999). Vygotskian theory and its application to language assessment: An overview for speech–language pathologists. *Contemporary Issues in Communication Science and Disorders, 26,* 111–118.

Justice, L. M., & Ezell, H. K. (2000). Enhancing children's print and word awareness through home-based parent intervention. *American Journal of Speech–Language Pathology, 9,* 257–269.

Justice, L. M., & Ezell, H. K. (2002). Use of storybook reading to increase print awareness in at-risk children. *American Journal of Speech–Language Pathology, 11,* 17–29.

Justice, L. M., & Ezell, H. K. (2004). Print referencing: An emergent literacy enhancement strategy and its clinical applications. *Language, Speech and Hearing Services in Schools, 35,* 185–193.

Justice, L. M., Kaderavek, J., Fan, X., Sofka, A., & Hunt, A. (2009). Accelerating preschoolers' early literacy development through teacher–child storybook reading. *Language, Speech, and Hearing Services in Schools, 40,* 67–85.

Justice, L. M., Meier, J., & Walpole, S. (2005). Learning new words from storybooks: Findings from an intervention with at-risk kindergartners. *Language, Speech, and Hearing Services in Schools, 36,* 17–32.

Justice, L. M., Pullen, P. C., & Pence, K. (2008). Influence of verbal and nonverbal references to print on preschoolers' visual attention to print during storybook reading. *Developmental Psychology, 44,* 855–866.

Justice, L. M., Skibbe, L., Canning, A., & Lankford, C. (2005). Preschoolers, print, and storybooks: An observational study using eye-gaze analysis. *Journal of Research in Reading, 28,* 229–243.

Keller, L. (2007). *Do unto otters.* New York: Henry Holt.

Keller, L. (2008). *The scrambled states of America talent show.* New York: Henry Holt.

Knapman, T. (2007). *Guess what I found in dragon wood?* New York: Bloomsbury U.S.A. Children's Books.

Kroll, S. (2005). *The biggest snowman ever.* New York: Scholastic.

Krosoczka, J. J. (2002). *Baghead.* New York: Random House.

Krull, K. (2003). *M is for music.* New York: Harcourt.

Landry, S., Miller-Loncar, C. L., Smith, K., & Swank, P. (1997). Predicting cognitive-language and social growth curves from early maternal behaviors in children at varying degrees of biological risk. *Developmental Psychology, 33,* 1040–1053.

Lemelin, J., Boivin, M., Forget-Dubois, N., Dionne, G., Séguin, J. R., Brendgen, M., et al.

(2007). The genetic–environmental etiology of cognitive school readiness and later academic achievement in early childhood. *Child Development, 78,* 1855–1869.

Le Neouanic, L. (2005). *Little smudge.* New York: Sterling.

Lionni, L. (1975). *A color of his own.* New York: Scholastic.

Lloyd, S. (2007). *Doctor meow's big emergency.* New York: Henry Holt.

Lloyd-Jones, S., & Heap, S. (2007). *How to be a baby.* New York: Schwartz & Wade Books.

London, J. (1992). *Froggy gets dressed.* New York: Puffin.

Lonigan, C. J., Anthony, J. L., Bloomfield, B. G., Dyer, S. M., & Samwel, C. S. (1999). Effects of two shared-reading interventions on emergent literacy skills of at-risk preschoolers. *Journal of Early Intervention, 22,* 306–322.

Lovelace, S., & Stewart, S. R. (2007). Increasing print awareness in preschoolers with language impairment with non-evocative print referencing. *Language, Speech, and Hearing Services in Schools, 38,* 16–30.

MacLachlan, P., & Charest, E. M. (2006). *Once I ate a pie.* New York: Joanna Cotter Books.

Martin, B. Jr., & Archambault, J. (1989). *Chicka chicka boom boom.* New York: Scholastic.

McCall, B. (2008). *Marveltown.* New York: Farrar, Straus & Giroux.

McGinty, A., & Justice, L. M. (2009). Predictors of print knowledge in children with specific language impairment: Experiential and developmental factors. *Journal of Speech, Language, and Hearing Research, 52,* 81–97.

McLeod, B. (2006). *Superhero ABC.* New York: HarperCollins.

McMullan, K. (2002). *I stink!* New York: HarperCollins.

Miranda, A. (1997). *To market, to market.* San Diego: Voyager Books.

Mitton, T. (2001). *Down by the cool of the pool.* New York: Orchard Books.

Moll, L. C. (1990). *Vygotsky and education: Instructional implications and applications of sociohistorical psychology.* Cambridge, NY: Cambridge University Press.

Monroe, C. (2008). *Monkey with a tool belt.* New York: Carolrhoda Books.

Morris, D., Bloodgood, J., Lomax, R. G., & Perney, J. (2003). Developmental steps in learning to read: A longitudinal study in kindergarten and first grade. *Reading Research Quarterly, 38,* 302–328.

Murphy, M. 1997). *I like it when ...* San Diego: Harcourt.

Murray, A. (2003). *The very sleepy sloth.* New York: Scholastic.

National Early Literacy Panel. (2008). *Report on a synthesis of early predictors of reading.* Louisville, KY: National Institute of Family Literacy.

Newman, B. J. (2007). *Tex and Sugar: A big city kitty ditty.* New York: Sterling.

Notari-Syverson, A., O'Connor, R., & Vadasy, P. F. (1998). *Ladders to literacy: A preschool activity book.* Baltimore: Brookes.

O'Connor, R. E., Notari-Syverson, A., & Vadasy, P. F. (1998). *Ladders to literacy : A kindergarten activity book.* Baltimore : Brookes.

O'Neil, A. (2008). *The worst best friend.* New York: Scholastic.

O'Neill, A. (2002). *The recess queen.* New York: Scholastic.

Page, G. (2008). *Bobo and the new neighbor.* New York: Bloomsbury U.S.A. Children's Books.

Page, N. (2008). *Do you do a didgeridoo?* Hertfordshire, UK: Make Believe Ideas.

Pandell, K. (1996). *Animal action ABC.* New York: Scholastic.

Park, B. (2008). *Ma! There's nothing to do here!* New York: Random House.

Pence, K., & Justice, L. M. (2007). *Language development: Theory to practice.* Upper Saddle River, NJ: Merrill/Prentice Hall.

Perlmutter, R. (2005). *Beethoven's wig.* Cambridge, MA: Rounder Books.

Petrill, S. A., Deater-Deckard, K., Schatschneider, C., & Davis, C. (2005). Measured environment influences on early reading: Evidence from an adoption study. *Scientific Studies of Reading, 9*(3), 237–260.

Petty, K. (2008). *Ha, ha, baby!* New York: Sterling.

Phillips, G., & McNaughton, S. (1990). The practice of storybook reading to preschool children in mainstream New Zealand families. *Reading Research Quarterly, 25*(3), 196–211.

Pianta, R. C., La Paro, K. M., & Hamre, B. K. (2004). *Classroom Assessment Scoring System (CLASS).* Charlottesville: University of Virginia.

Pilkey, D. (1994). *Dog breath.* New York: Scholastic.

Portis, A. (2006). *Not a box.* New York: HarperCollins.

Provensen, A. (2003). *A day in the life of Murphy.* New York: Simon & Schuster Books for Young Readers.

Purcell-Gates, V., Jacobson, E., & Degener, S. (2004). *Print literacy development: Uniting cognitive and social practice theories.* Cambridge, MA: Harvard University Press.

Riley, L. (1997). *Mouse mess.* New York: Blue Sky Press.

Roberts, J., Jergens, J., & Burchinal, M. (2005). The role of home literacy practices in preschool children's language and emergent literacy skills. *Journal of Speech, Language, and Hearing Research, 48*(2), 345–359.

Root, P. (2001). *Rattletrap car.* Cambridge, MA: Candlewick Press.

Rosen, M., & Oxenbury, H. (1989). *We're going on a bear hunt.* New York: Aladdin.

Rosenthal, A. K. (2006). *Cookies.* New York: HarperCollins.

Rosoff, M. & Blackall, S. (2005). *Meet wild boars.* New York: Henry Holt.

Schaefer, C. L. (1996). *The squiggle.* New York: Crown.

Schatschneider, C., Fletcher, J. M., Francis, D. J., Carlson, C., & Foorman, B. R. (2004). Kindergarten prediction of reading skills: A longitudinal comparative analysis. *Journal of Educational Psychology, 96,* 265–282.

Schuele, C. M., Justice, L. M., Cabell, S., Knighton, K., Kingery, B., & Lee, M. (2008). Field-based evaluation of two-tiered phonological awareness intervention. *Early Education and Development, 19,* 726–752.

Scieszka, J. (2008). *Smash! Crash!* New York: Simon & Schuster Books for Young Readers.

Sénéchal, M., LeFevre, J.-A., Thomas, E. M., & Daley, K. E. (1998). Differential effects of home literacy experiences on the development of oral and written language. *Reading Research Quarterly, 33*(1), 96–116.

Shannon, D. (2002). *David gets in trouble.* New York: Blue Sky Press.

Shannon, D. (2008). *Too many toys.* New York: Blue Sky Press.

Shea, B. (2008). *Dinosaur vs. bedtime.* New York: Hyperion Books for Children.

Shields, G. (2008). *Dogfish.* New York: Atheneum Books for Young Readers.

Sierra, J. (2004). *Wild about books.* New York: Knopf.

Skibbe, L. E., Justice, L. M., McGinty, A., & Zucker, T. (2008). Relations among maternal literacy beliefs, home literacy practices, and the emergent literacy skills of preschoolers with language impairment. *Early Education and Development, 19,* 68–88.

Slate, J. (1996). *Miss Bindergarten gets ready for kindergarten.* New York: Dutton.

Smee, N. (2006). *Clip-clop.* New York: Boxer Books.

Smolkin, L. B., Conlon, A., & Yaden, D. B. (1988). Print salient illustrations in children's picture books: The emergence of written language awareness. In J. E. Readance & R. S. Baldwin (Eds.), *Dialogues in literacy research: Thirty-seventh yearbook of the National Reading Conference* (pp. 59–68). Chicago: National Reading Conference.

Snow, C. E. (1983). Literacy and language: Relationships during the preschool years. *Harvard Educational Review, 53*, 165–189.

Snow, C. E., Burns, M. S., & Griffin, P. (1998). *Preventing reading difficulties in young children*. Washington, DC: National Academy Press.

Soman, D. & Davis, J. (2008). *Ladybug girl*. New York: Dial Books for Young Readers.

Stanovich, P. J., & Stanovich, K. E. (2003). *Using research and reason in education: How teachers can use scientifically based research to make curricular instructional decisions.* Washington, DC: Partnership for Reading.

Stevens, A. & Hills, T. (2007). *Waking up Wendell*. New York: Schwartz & Wade Books.

Storch, S., & Whitehurst, G. (2002). Oral language and code-related precursors to reading: Evidence from a longitudinal structural model. *Developmental Psychology, 38*, 934–947.

Vukelich, C. (1994). Effects of play interventions on young children's reading of environmental print. *Early Childhood Research Quarterly, 9*, 153–170.

Thayer, E. L. (2000). *Casey at the bat*. Brooklyn, NY: Handprint Books.

Thomas, H. & Bok, C. (2008). *The great whitehouse breakout*. New York: Dial Books for Young Readers.

Thomas, S. M. (2008). *A cold winter's good knight*. New York: Dutton Children's Books.

Tolhurst, M. (1990). *Somebody and the three Blairs*. New York: Orchard Books.

Tyler, J., & Hawthorn, P. (1996). *There's a dragon at my school*. London: Usborne.

Urbanovic, J. (2007). *Duck at the door*. New York: HarperCollins.

Urbanovic, J. (2008). *Duck soup*. New York: HarperCollins.

Vail, R. (2008). *Jibberwillies at night*. New York: Scholastic Press.

Vygotsky, L. S. (1978). *Mind in society: The development of higher psychological processes.* Cambridge, MA: Harvard University Press. (Original work published 1930)

Vygotksy, L. S. (1986). *Thought and language* (A. Kozulin, Ed.). Cambridge, MA: MIT Press. (Original work published 1934)

Ward, J. (2007). *There was a coyote who swallowed a flea*. New York: Rising Moon.

Ward, N. (2008). *The nicest naughty fairy*. London: Meadowside Children's Books.

Wells, R. (1997). *Bunny cakes*. New York: Scholastic.

Whitehurst, G. J., Falco, F. L., Lonigan, C. J., Fischel, J. E., DeBaryshe, B. D., Valdez-Menchaca, M. C., et al. (1988). Accelerating language development through picture book reading. *Developmental Psychology, 24*, 552–559.

Whitehurst, G. J., & Lonigan, C. J. (1998). Child development and emergent literacy. *Child Development, 69*, 848–872.

Willems, M. (2004). *Knuffle bunny*. New York: Hyperion Books for Children.

Willems, M. (2005). *Leonardo the terrible monster*. New York: Hyperion Books for Children.

Williams, V. B. (1990). *More, more, more, said the baby*. New York: Greenwillow Books.

Wing, N. (2001). *The night before kindergarten*. New York: Grosset & Dunlap.

Wood, D., & Middleton, D. (1975). A study of assisted problem-solving. *British Journal of Psychology, 66*(2), 181–191.

Wright, M. (2008). *Jake starts school*. New York: Feiwel and Friends.

Yaden, D. B., Smolkin, L. B., & Conlon, A. (1989). Preschoolers' questions about pictures, print conventions, and story text during reading aloud at home. *Reading Research Quarterly, 24*(2), 188–214.

Zechel, E. (2008). *Is there a mouse in the baby's room?* New York: Lark Books.

Zucker, T., Justice, L. M., & Piasta, S. (2009). Preschool teachers' references to print during classroom-based large-group shared reading. *Language, Speech, and Hearing Services in Schools, 40*, 376–392.

Index